The Psychology of Vampires
David Cohen

The Psychology of Chess
Fernand Gobet

The Psychology of Music
Susan Hallam

**The Psychology of
Weather**
Trevor Harley

Doreen Rosenthal and Susan M. Moore

**The Psychology of School
Bullying**
Peter Smith

The Psychology of Celebrity
Gayle Stever

For further information about this series please visit
www.thepsychologyofeverything.co.uk

THE PSYCHOLOGY OF DRIVING

Do we become better or worse drivers as we age? Why do we indulge in risky behaviour when driving? Will technology remove the human role in driving forever?

The Psychology of Driving is a fascinating introduction into the psychological factors at play when people get behind the wheel. Exploring the role of personality traits and cognitive functions, such as attention in driving, the book considers why human error is most often to blame in road accidents, and how we can improve driver safety. The book debunks the myth that men are better drivers than women and considers why some people indulge in knowingly risky behaviour on the road, including using mobile phones and drink/drug-driving.

In a time when driverless cars are becoming a reality, The Psychology of Driving shows us how human behaviour and decisions can still affect our lives on the road.

Graham Hole is a Senior Lecturer in Psychology at the University of Sussex, UK.

THE PSYCHOLOGY OF EVERYTHING

The Psychology of Everything is a series of books which debunk the myths and pseudo-science surrounding some of life's biggest questions.

The series explores the hidden psychological factors that drive us, from our sub-conscious desires and aversions, to the innate social instincts handed to us across the generations. Accessible, informative, and always intriguing, each book is written by an expert in the field, examining how research-based knowledge compares with popular wisdom, and illustrating the potential of psychology to enrich our understanding of humanity and modern life.

Applying a psychological lens to an array of topics and contemporary concerns – from sex to addiction to conspiracy theories – The Psychology of Everything will make you look at everything in a new way.

Titles in the series:

The Psychology of Grief
Richard Gross

The Psychology of Sex
Meg-John Barker

The Psychology of Dieting
Jane Ogden

The Psychology of Performance
Stewart T. Cotterill

The Psychology of Trust
Ken J. Rotenberg

The Psychology of Working Life
Toon Taris

The Psychology of Conspiracy Theories
Jan-Willem van Prooijen

The Psychology of Addiction
Jenny Svanberg

The Psychology of Fashion
Carolyn Mair

The Psychology of Gardening
Harriet Gross

The Psychology of Gender
Gary W. Wood

The Psychology of Climate Change
Geoffrey Beattie

THE PSYCHOLOGY OF DRIVING

GRAHAM HOLE

Routledge
Taylor & Francis Group

LONDON AND NEW YORK

First published 2019
by Routledge
2 Park Square, Milton Park, Abingdon, Oxon OX14 4RN

and by Routledge
711 Third Avenue, New York, NY 10017

Routledge is an imprint of the Taylor & Francis Group, an informa business

British Library Cataloguing-in-Publication Data
A catalogue record for this book is available from the British Library

Library of Congress Cataloging-in-Publication Data
A catalog record for this book has been requested

ISBN: 978-1-138-69957-1 (hbk)
ISBN: 978-1-138-69958-8 (pbk)
ISBN: 978-1-315-51653-0 (ebk)

Typeset in Joanna
by Apex CoVantage, LLC

Printed and bound by CPI Group (UK) Ltd, Croydon, CR0 4Y

In memory of my mum, Joyce Alice Hole

CONTENTS

PREFACE

There is a disease that kills roughly 1.25 million people *every year* and causes harm to around 50 million more, often leaving them with life-changing disabilities. It's the ninth most common cause of death in the world, and it's the leading cause of death for 15- to 29-year-olds. And the really sad thing is that it's largely preventable.

Since you're reading this book, you've probably guessed what this disease is: road accidents. These statistics come from the World Health Organisation's *Global Status Report on Road Safety, 2015*. Great Britain is one of the safest countries in the world for driving – only Norway and Sweden are safer. Even so, in 2016 the Department for Transport reports that there were 1,792 deaths on the road in Britain, 24,101 serious accidents and perhaps as many as 700,000 accidents in total. That's five deaths on the roads every day.

Psychology is relevant to all this because the vast majority of road accidents are due to human error, not mechanical failure. Drivers crash for many reasons. They fail to see each other; they take risks, such as overtaking in silly places or driving too fast for the conditions; and they drive while affected by alcohol, drugs, lack of sleep or while they are distracted by their phones. Sometimes they crash because they get angry or frustrated with one another. A minority of elderly drivers crash because they can no longer cope with the mental and physical demands of driving. Perception, attention, fatigue, aggression, risk perception, ageing and so on are all issues that have been studied extensively by psychologists, often for many decades. Psychologists know an awful lot that is relevant to understanding how humans manage to drive and why sometimes they fail.

This book can only be a brief introduction to psychological research that is relevant to driving. There are literally thousands of research papers on each of the topics covered in this book. My emphasis will be on *cognitive* psychology (specifically perception and attention), partly as a reflection of my own background but also because we are very visual animals and driving is a very visual business. However, social psychologists also play a very important role in understanding how and why we drive like we do. Social psychology deals with topics such as attitude formation, attitude change and risk perception, and knowledge of these topics is essential for understanding why drivers take risks and how they can be persuaded to drive more safely.

This book is intended for anyone who has an interest in driving, and I hope there is something here for everyone. Driving is a topic that many people have strong opinions about, but opinions are not necessarily based on good evidence. Psychology is a science: it uses the scientific method to investigate issues. Psychologists are trained to obtain and assess evidence as objectively as they can. "Intuitive plausibility" has no place in psychology. The topic of driving abounds with claims that seem plausible, such as "car drivers pull out on motorcyclists at junctions because motorcycles are hard to see", "old drivers are involved in more accidents because their eyesight is bad" and "mobile telephones are safe as long as the driver has both hands on the driving wheel". As we shall see, there is little evidence for any of these statements: in each case, the truth is more complicated and more interesting.

If psychology is so relevant to driving, why do non-psychologists know so little about it? Part of the problem is that although there is a huge scientific literature on driving and related topics, much of it is rather inaccessible to the non-specialist, because of the jargon and statistics used. Hence my intention in the following pages is to use as little jargon as possible, while at the same time trying to avoid over-simplifying or trivialising the arguments. It is my firm belief that anything – no matter how complicated – can be explained if one takes enough time and trouble. I sincerely hope I have succeeded in this.

I'd like to take this opportunity to thank the following people for their help with this book: Kevan Phillips, Euan Phillips, Sarah Laurence, Jess Marshall and Neville Stanton.

1

PERCEPTION AND ATTENTION IN DRIVING

INTRODUCTION

Visual perception is clearly very important for driving: try driving for any length of time with your eyes shut and you'll see what I mean. Many accidents seem to involve "perceptual" errors. Every year in the UK, a contributory factor in about 45% of reported road accidents is that a driver or rider "failed to look properly". The second most common factor, accounting for a further 25% of accidents, is "driver/rider failed to judge other person's path or speed". In many collisions, at least one of the drivers claimed that he or she failed to see the other vehicle beforehand. The victims of these "looked but failed to see" accidents are often cyclists and motorcyclists.

Often, it's suggested that these accidents – especially the ones involving two-wheelers – are due to limitations in people's eyesight (in the sense of the sharpness of vision that's measured by an eyechart). Sometimes it's claimed they are due to the visual system's "deficiencies", such as the fact that our retinal image is "poor" or because we are "blind" during eye movements. If you actually understand how the visual system works, you realise that none of these claims is true. Any problems really lie in the driver's brain, not the eyeballs. To explain what I mean by this, I need to tell you a bit about the visual system and what it's designed to do.

VISUAL PERCEPTION IS REALLY DIFFICULT!

While you are driving, your brain rapidly and apparently effortlessly builds up an impression of a stable, richly detailed 3D world, from a constantly changing array of shapes and edges. Your brain decides which contours belong together as "objects", even when one object is partially obscured by another (such as a pedestrian peeking out from behind a bus). It distinguishes between different kinds of movement – movement produced by your vehicle, by that pedestrian and by your eyes rapidly moving from looking in the mirror to scanning the road ahead.

To achieve this feat, a phenomenal amount of information-processing goes on behind the scenes. The eye is not a camera; it is just part of a set of neural systems that use light reflected from objects in order to acquire important information about the world. Each eye produces an upside-down (yes, really!), dim, blurry and shaky retinal image, about the size of a postage stamp. No one is looking at that image; it's just the starting point for the processes underlying visual perception. The eye transmits information to the brain in the form of patterns of electrical impulses, which the brain then interprets.

Our subjective impressions give us a very false idea of how our perceptual processes actually operate. Did you notice the intermittent darkness produced by the dozen or so blinks that you made while you read this page or the way your eyes moved jerkily along each sentence? In "change-blindness" demonstrations, observers have to spot the difference between two images that are displayed alternately. It is surprisingly difficult to find even quite major differences, unless you are looking directly at the change as it happens. The change-blindness technique simulates what happens every time you move your eyes: your brain discards most of the information obtained from where you were looking previously, retaining only the gist of the scene. Everywhere you look, the scene appears highly detailed, but this is what Ronald Rensink and others have called the "grand illusion" of visual consciousness. You're unaware that where you looked previously is represented only very coarsely by the brain – because you are not looking there now.

The brain is faced with a huge problem: for visual information to be of any use, it has to be interpreted very rapidly, but there is a vast amount of information in any scene. Therefore the brain needs to be very selective. It is optimised for detecting *change* of some kind. Changes in space or time have biological relevance; constant states do not. It is the abrupt change produced by the edge of a cliff that you need to worry about, not the flat expanse of grassland leading up to it.

At all levels, from the retina up to "higher" brain regions, the visual system is beautifully designed for efficient information-acquisition. Firstly, only a very small part of the scene in front of you is analysed in any detail. Fine-detail vision is confined to a central region of each retina, called the fovea. Beyond this tiny region, just 1.5 millimetres (mm) in diameter, acuity (sharpness of vision) becomes progressively poorer, so that in our extreme peripheral vision, we can perceive little more than a vague sensation of movement (see Figure 1.1).

The lack of acuity in peripheral vision is not a problem in practice, because when we look at anything, eye movements ensure that its image falls upon the fovea. Normal vision consists of brief fixations (about three per second), linked by eye movements (mainly rapid, large-scale movements called "saccades"). A shift of fixation occurs either because something attracts our attention or on the basis of our knowledge and expectations about where it would be useful to look next (more on this later).

Figure 1.1 A demonstration of how visual acuity deteriorates in peripheral vision. What the camera sees (left) and what the visual system sees (right), when fixating the car. Thanks to Stuart Anstis for the Photoshop algorithm that produced the right-hand image.

This is a brilliantly elegant way to solve the problem of information overload. We don't need to store the entire "outside world" in our heads; we just sample information from the world as and when we need it, by moving our eyes to where that information might be located.

Another way in which the brain copes with information overload is by processing visual information within only a restricted range of what is potentially available. Any scene contains information at different levels of detail. These are reflected in the "spatial frequency" content of the image, how often a pattern changes from light to dark as one moves across it in any particular direction. High spatial frequencies contain information about fine detail in an image (such as the contours produced by the leaves on a tree). Low spatial frequencies carry information about larger-scale changes in an image (such as the gross difference between a tree and its background). Figure 1.2 shows the results of filtering an image to selectively remove the high spatial frequencies.

Different tasks may require analysis at different spatial scales. For many driving-related tasks (such as rapid scene analysis, lane

Figure 1.2 Image filtered so that only low spatial frequencies are present.

guidance and collision-avoidance), we don't actually need fine-detail (high spatial frequency) information; fairly coarse (medium- to low frequency) information will suffice. The car in Figure 1.2 remains easily identifiable despite the loss of information about its details.

You might be wondering how I can argue that eyesight limitations are not the cause of accidents when I've spent so much time describing the visual system's limitations. That's because these "deficiencies" are only a problem if you are locked into the misconception that vision somehow consists of us "seeing" our retinal image. The retinal image might be fairly rubbish, but *seeing* is not.

Here's an illustration of how much processing goes on and what it can achieve. Each eye contains 127 million light-sensitive cells (photoreceptors). Seven million of these are "cones", providing your fine-detail colour vision in daylight. The rest are "rods", providing you with coarser monochromatic vision in twilight conditions. Your sharpest vision is primarily based on just 200,000 cones in the very centre of each fovea. However the resolution of the visual system is far better than you would expect on the basis of the size of the photoreceptors themselves. The smallest detectable misalignment between two vertical lines is a *tenth of the diameter of the smallest cone in this region*, and you can see an offset this small even when the lines are moving across the retina! Instances of "visual hyperacuity" like this demonstrate how much processing is going on in the brain. Electrical impulses from the retina are only the starting point in a set of processes designed to extract useful information about the world.

THE ROLE OF HYPOTHESES AND SCHEMAS IN VISUAL PERCEPTION

Human information-processing seems to rely heavily on "schemas". These are generalisations that are abstracted from a number of specific instances of an activity. Schemas can operate at different levels. At a low level, there may be schemas for actions such as emerging from a junction, stopping at traffic lights, changing lanes and so on – activities that a driver has performed many thousands of times, even though each occasion differs in its details. At a higher level, there may be schemas for regular journeys, such as going from the house to the supermarket or picking up the children from school – again, highly repetitive events which usually differ only in the details from one instance to another.

Schemas enable us to predict what is likely to happen and respond efficiently as a result. Given that driving is such a predictable and repetitive activity most of the time, schemas – and the expectations that they generate – probably play an important role in determining drivers' behaviour.

The existence of perceptual schemas is supported by recent work on "predictive coding". For some years, the dominant view has been that perceptual processing progresses solely from "lower" to "higher" brain regions. The idea is that it starts with an analysis of elementary perceptual properties, such as detecting edges. "Higher" regions then integrate these into more abstract representations of objects. Finally, these representations are linked to conceptual knowledge about the objects and their significance to the viewer. However, recent neurophysiological research shows that information also flows in the *opposite* direction, down from "high-level" to "low-level" areas. Higher areas may actively test competing "hypotheses" about what incoming information represents, modulating the activity of the lower areas in order to maximise the amount of information coming up that would enable a choice to be made between these alternative hypotheses. In short, the brain uses its knowledge about the world in order to interpret sensory data. Most of the time, this is a very efficient strategy – as long as the hypotheses are appropriate.

Let's return to the accident data at the start of this chapter. As I mentioned, many accidents are collisions at junctions; for example, a driver pulls out from a side-road into the path of an oncoming vehicle that has right of way. The offending driver often claims to have looked in the appropriate direction but failed to see the other vehicle. Why do these "looked but failed to see" (LBFS) accidents occur? The most obvious explanation is that the oncoming vehicle was hard to see, in sensory terms. This view appears to be supported by the fact that motorcyclists and cyclists are often the victims in this type of accident. It's argued that two-wheelers are small and hence difficult to see and so it's understandable that a driver might fail to detect them while trying to emerge from a junction. A closer look at the evidence suggests that LBFS accidents are not caused by limitations of the offending driver's low-level visual system. Instead they are due to failures of the more "cognitive" systems involved in attention, which are affected by the driver's expectations about what he or she is likely to see.

You can often understand how something works by seeing how it goes wrong. By looking at LBFS accidents more closely, we can gain some insight into how perception normally works during driving.

TWO FACTORS THAT AFFECT ATTENTION

Because we possess fine-detail vision only in a small part of our visual field, we have to direct our attention to various parts of our surroundings in turn, rather than trying to perceive the entire scene at once. There are two main influences on this process. Attention can be captured automatically and involuntarily by external stimuli, such as a sudden movement or noise. Attention can also be influenced by internal cues: it can be goal-driven, directed to something voluntarily and consciously.

This distinction between two types of determinant of attention is mirrored in discussions of visibility, or "conspicuity" as it's usually referred to by researchers. Something with high "sensory conspicuity", such as a bright object against a dark background, attracts attention even though the observer is not specifically looking for it. "Cognitive conspicuity" relates to the capacity of an object to be detected if the observer is actively searching for it. This latter type of conspicuity depends on the observer's psychological state as well as the properties of the object itself. Sensory conspicuity is based more on "data-driven", "bottom-up" processing; cognitive conspicuity relies more on conceptually driven, "top-down" processing.

The two types of conspicuity need not coincide. For example, road signs giving route information are designed to have high sensory conspicuity: they are large, bright and positioned to be easily seen (well, usually!). For a driver who needs to know that route information, the sign might also possess cognitive conspicuity: the driver is actively looking for that particular information. For a driver who knows the route well, the sign is irrelevant and so it might not even be noticed, despite its sensory conspicuity.

As well as the nature of the stimuli that attract attention, another aspect of attention that needs to be considered is its breadth: subjectively, we feel we can vary the distribution of our attention, from covering a wide area to being tightly focused. A popular model of attention has been the "zoom lens" model. This suggests that attention is like a searchlight, ranging over a scene, and that the breadth of the "beam" can be varied from narrow to wide. Another popular idea is that under stress, attention shrinks towards the point of fixation – a sort of cognitive "tunnel vision". This implies that the further something is from the point of fixation, the less likely it is to be noticed.

WHAT DO DRIVERS LOOK AT?

One way to try to find out what drivers are attending to is to record their eye movements. This method assumes that what a driver is looking at is what he or she is attending to. As we shall see, there is a lot of evidence that this is not always the case, but eye-tracking gives us a rough idea of how drivers allocate their attention.

Studies by Ronald Mourant and Thomas Rockwell in the 1970s found interesting differences in drivers' eye movements as a result of experience. Compared to experienced drivers, novice drivers tended to search a smaller part of the scene, closer to the car; they tended to have a narrower horizontal search pattern; and they generally made less use of their mirrors. Novices' fixations tended to be longer than those of experienced drivers, and they made more pursuit tracking eye movements (i.e., followed objects with their eyes). Novices also seemed less able to use information from their peripheral vision in order to steer the vehicle.

More recently, Geoffrey Underwood and his colleagues at Nottingham University have performed a large number of studies comparing the fixation patterns of novice and experienced drivers, both in the laboratory and in real-life driving conditions. Their findings extend Mourant and Rockwell's, additionally showing that novices and experienced drivers behave differently on different types of road. Experienced drivers generally have a broader sweep of attention, but they vary the width of their search depending on the circumstances. They have a wider spread of fixations on dual carriageways, both horizontally and vertically, than on other types of road. Their fixation durations are shorter on demanding roads, possibly so that they can sample more of the scene. Novices show little variation in their fixation behaviour, regardless of the difficulty of the road being driven.

A study by Shinoda, Hayhoe and Shrivastava (2001) provides a good illustration of how experienced drivers actively sample their visual environment in order to obtain information as and when it is actually needed. Information that is directly relevant to the task is acquired, and irrelevant information is ignored. Participants "drove" around a computer-generated town in a driving simulator. Occasionally, a "no parking" sign briefly turned into a "stop" sign. Detection of the change depended on the driver's knowledge of where stop signs are normally located and their knowledge of when they should be looking for it. For example, they were much less likely to notice that the sign had changed when it was located mid-block than when it was located just before a junction.

Eye-movement recording studies demonstrate that fixation patterns are determined by an interplay of both external ("bottom-up") and internal ("top-down") factors. Drivers' fixation patterns (and by implication, their allocation of attention) depend a lot on past experience: drivers usually know where to look, what to look for and when to look for it. "Top-down" control of attentional allocation like this is highly efficient, but it also carries a penalty – a strategy of looking for what you expect to find may mean you sometimes overlook what is actually there. As the psychologist Richard Gregory once put it, "[W]e not only believe what we see, but we see what we believe".

MOTORCYCLE CONSPICUITY

About 75% of motorcycle accidents involve collision with another road-user (ACEM 2009). In many of these collisions, a vehicle emerged from a junction or turned across the motorcyclist's path (Figure 1.3).

When the offending drivers are asked why they failed to give way, they often say they "looked but failed to see" the motorcyclist. These kinds of statements have been taken at face value by many researchers, because it seems common sense that motorcycles are hard to see. The fundamental problem must be that the small size of motorcycles makes it difficult for the visual system to detect them. This has led to lots of research into ways to "improve" motorcyclists' sensory conspicuity to other road-users, generally by using daytime headlights or fluorescent clothing to make the motorcycle brighter. However, a truly scientific approach to this issue reveals

Figure 1.3 A common type of motorcycle accident: a driver emerges from a junction and collides with a motorcyclist who has right of way on the main road.

that this line of thinking is fallacious. Let's consider the evidence step by step.

1. What do drivers really mean when they say they "failed to see" the motorcycle?

When a driver says, "I looked, but I didn't see the motorcyclist", it has often been taken to mean that the motorcycle *could not be seen*. However, this is an interpretation that goes beyond what the driver is actually saying. All we really know for certain is that the driver claimed to have looked in the direction of the oncoming motorcyclist but for some unspecified reason was *not aware* of the motorcyclist's presence. In science, it's always important to distinguish between the actual data that you have and the theoretical interpretation of those data, but many researchers on this topic have confused the two. The conventional interpretation of the driver's statement about what happened is just that – it's an interpretation produced because the researcher has already made the assumption that motorcyclists are physically difficult to detect.

2. Are motorcycles really hard to see?

It's true that, placed at the same distance from the viewer, motorcycles have a much smaller frontal area than cars or trucks. However, being *harder* to detect is not the same as being *difficult* to detect. Many of these collisions occur in broad daylight, good weather and crucially, *when the motorcyclist is so close to the driver who pulls out that neither can avert a collision*. Under these conditions, motorcycles are well above the sensory threshold for detection: they produce a very large image on the driver's retina, which should *not* be hard to detect (see Figure 1.4). Small things which are close to you produce a big image on the retina; big things which are far away produce a small image. Hold your thumb close to your eye and you can blot out the sun, even though the sun is nearly 865 million miles wide. It's the size of the image on the retina that counts, not the size of the object itself. Nearby motorcycles are big!

Figure 1.4 Although motorcycles are physically smaller than other vehicles, it's the retinal image size that counts – a nearby motorcycle's retinal image is bigger than a distant car's. (The car's image has been cut out and placed next to the motorcycle to make the point).

3. Why can some people detect motorcycles but not others?

Car drivers who know motorcyclists or are motorcyclists themselves ("dual drivers") are less likely to pull out in front of motorcycles (Magazzù, Comelli and Marinoni 2006; ACEM 2009). It's unlikely there are systematic differences in eyesight between these groups and people who don't know any motorcyclists. It's more likely that they search for motorcycles more effectively than non-motorcyclists before they emerge from a junction. If they can see motorcycles, then anyone should be able to – so poor sensory conspicuity cannot be the main explanation for LBFS accidents.

4. Drivers pull out in front of "conspicuous" things too.

Although "looked but failed to see" accidents are the most common type of accident for motorcyclists and cyclists, drivers sometimes pull out in front of large vehicles too, such as trucks and buses. No one would claim these are below sensory thresholds for detection. Drivers have even been known to drive into the back of a parked police car and claim they didn't see it beforehand (Langham et al. 2002)! It would be difficult to argue that police cars are hard to see, given their flashing lights and high-visibility markings.

5. But – daytime headlights and fluorescent clothing may make it easier to detect motorcyclists.

The evidence for any benefits of conspicuity aids is actually quite weak. Studies of motorcycle accident statistics in various countries, before and after compulsory daytime motorcycle headlight laws were introduced, have generally found little effect. Experimental studies in the 1970s that supposedly found benefits for conspicuity enhancements are still widely cited today but actually had serious methodological flaws that invalidate their conclusions. An in-depth study of 921 European motorcycle accidents (ACEM, 2009) found that 69% of these motorcyclists were using their headlight at the time of their crash, suggesting that headlight use didn't help them to be detected by other road-users.

Even if conspicuity aids did enhance motorcyclists' visibility to other road-users, this is not evidence that the aids are remedying a *sensory* deficit. Again, this confuses the data (improvement in detectability) with the interpretation. The naive interpretation is that the conspicuity aids are improving the sensory "signal" produced by the motorcyclist, so that it is now above some threshold for detection. An alternative interpretation is that they improve the motorcyclist's *cognitive* conspicuity.

THE ROLE OF EXPECTATIONS IN MOTORCYCLE CONSPICUITY (AND DRIVING GENERALLY)

There is overwhelming evidence that motorcycles are simply not hard to see in sensory terms. So why do drivers fail to detect them (or parked police cars, for that matter)? Probably because they have faulty expectations or inappropriate schemas. Perhaps drivers at junctions largely see what they *expect* to see: approaching cars and trucks. Motorcyclists and cyclists are comparatively rare, representing less than 1% of traffic. Because they are unexpected, information about their presence does not reach the driver's conscious awareness. In other words, the LBFS accident arises from problems of cognitive conspicuity, not sensory conspicuity.

Evidence that expectations affect two-wheelers' conspicuity comes from a number of sources. Lisa Tyrrell and I showed that after repeated exposure to photographic slides of headlight-using motorcyclists, participants were much slower to respond to a slide of an unlit motorcyclist – even though he was nearby (and therefore large on the retina). Some participants failed to detect him altogether. Expectations seem to have engendered a perceptual "set" or "schema".

A highly influential model of human information-processing was put forward by Donald Norman and Tim Shallice. Their idea is that much of our routine behaviour is handled fairly automatically by a "contention scheduling system" that uses environmental triggers to activate schemas (see Chapter 2 for a discussion of this in relation to mobile-phone-use). Experienced drivers will have emerged from junctions many times and so are likely to have a well-developed schema for the activity. Repeated exposure to headlight-using motorcyclists may have encouraged our participants to look for a headlight rather than a motorcycle, so that this simple perceptual attribute was enough to activate the schema of "oncoming motorcyclist". More important, the *absence* of a lit headlight led to this schema *not* being activated, even though a motorcyclist was actually present. Driving often involves considerable time pressure, especially at junctions. One way to cope might be to use minimal cues as a basis for action, rather than engaging in a lengthy detailed analysis of the scene.

Environmental triggers could be developed through experience and normally would be an effective substitute for a detailed perceptual analysis of the driver's surroundings. Thus a headlight might signify "motorcycle", a flashing light might signify "bicycle" and a horizontal blob might be enough to signify "car". Detecting these triggers is all that would be needed in order to make judgements about whether or not it is safe to emerge from a junction. However, an unfortunate consequence of relying on environmental triggers is that if they are missing, drivers might fail to detect a vehicle even if it were well above perceptual thresholds (as in the case of the nearby unlit motorcyclist in our experiment).

These findings suggest that daytime headlight use might improve motorcyclists' conspicuity but not because it remedies a deficit in sensory conspicuity. Instead, it improves *cognitive* conspicuity – by providing a cue that drivers already associate with motorcycles or by providing a signal that is out of the ordinary and so triggers a direction of attention to the motorcyclist that might not otherwise have occurred.

This explanation also accounts for why drivers sometimes crash into parked police cars. In the Langham et al. study briefly mentioned earlier, it was found that these collisions tended to happen when the police car was parked in a straight line. On a high-speed road, drivers need to pay relatively little attention to the other traffic, as it's all going in the same direction and at roughly the same speed. Stationary vehicles within one's own lane are almost never encountered on these kinds of roads. Therefore, if a driver sees a car ahead, it is reasonable to assume that it is moving in the same direction as he or she is. A stationary police car activates the same schema as a moving one. Looming (rapid expansion of the retinal image of the police car) doesn't become an obvious cue to the fact that the car is stationary until it's too late to take evasive action. We found that police cars were noticed quicker if they were parked at a 45-degree angle to the highway. At this orientation, the parked police car gives off a strong signal that something is out of the ordinary – that it isn't just another moving vehicle.

Taken together, these experiments provide good evidence that drivers may sometimes fail to see even objectively highly conspicuous objects. High sensory conspicuity is not always enough to guarantee detection.

The idea that potentially important stimuli in the driver's environment can go completely unnoticed is supported by the phenomenon of "Inattentional Blindness". People can be looking directly at something and yet be unaware of its existence because it is not being attended to – even when the unattended stimulus is present in central vision for a prolonged amount of time. Simons and Chabris' (1999) demonstration of this has caught the public's imagination: participants watching a video of people playing a ball-passing game are so intent on paying attention to who passes the ball to whom that they often fail to notice a person in a gorilla suit walk amongst the ball-players and beat his chest!

Inattentional Blindness is a plausible explanation for many "looked but failed to see" accidents. A driver trying to emerge from a junction is expecting to see cars and hence is specifically looking for them in order to make a perceptual judgement about them (i.e., whether they are far enough away for it to be safe to pull out). If attention is focused on this as the primary task, it is likely that the driver might not consciously see a motorcyclist or cyclist as a result, even if the other person is close to the point of fixation.

CONCLUSION

Visual perception is an incredibly difficult task for the brain to achieve, and we are asking a great deal of our visual systems when we drive. As the Swedish psychologist Kåre Rumar pointed out, we drive at high speed using a primate visual system that evolved for navigating our ancestors through the savannah at 10 to 15 miles per hour. The primary role of the visual system is to supply rapid but often rough-and-ready answers to the question "What's around me and how useful or dangerous is it to me?" As a consequence, our visual abilities may sometimes let us down when it comes to driving.

Attention is a vital and integral aspect of visual processing. It determines what we see, when we see it and even if we become aware of it at all. It is allocated on the basis of a complex interplay between internal and external factors. On the one hand, it's important to give a high priority to directing attention towards stimuli which have high levels of sensory conspicuity by virtue of their brightness, sudden onset, and so on. However, it also makes sense to allocate attention on the basis of past experience, rather than starting from scratch every time a new scene is encountered. It's also sensible to attend to stimuli which are likely to be relevant to the task at hand. This means that sensory conspicuity is not the sole determinant of attention (and hence awareness) for drivers; "internal" factors can be just as important and may even override sensory conspicuity.

Research suggests that many accidents attributed to "sensory" perceptual failures are really due to problems with attention. This is not merely an academic distinction. A failure to appreciate that sensory conspicuity does not guarantee conscious detection has led to many researchers going down a blind alley when it comes to researching the problem of motorcycle conspicuity, focusing on ways to make motorcycles brighter rather than trying to find methods of ensuring they reach drivers' awareness. It has also led to unfortunate policy decisions, such as the European Union's decision to introduce compulsory daytime headlights for cars. This may have decreased the safety of motorcyclists, by removing the unique "shorthand code" that signifies "motorcycle present". In line with this argument, Cavallo and Pinto (2012) found that car daytime running lights reduced the detectability of motorcyclists, cyclists and pedestrians.

A skilled driver will be "reading" the road ahead, using a combination of visual information and past experience to anticipate what is likely to happen next. Anticipation buys time for responding – quick as our reactions are, it would be very difficult to drive above walking pace if one had to continually respond to events as they actually happened. However, as we have seen, there may sometimes be penalties for driving on the basis of what one *expects* to see, rather than what is actually present.

2

DISTRACTED DRIVING

INTRODUCTION

"Infotainment" is big business. Car manufacturers are competing with each other to pack their cars with technology that facilitates communication with the external world. Most new cars enable the driver to talk on a mobile phone via a Bluetooth connection to the car's audio system, use satellite navigation and access the Internet. Some enable the driver to send and receive emails via a text-to-speech interface. How distracting is all this technology?

DEFINING "DISTRACTION"

Car manufacturers claim their infotainment systems are "safe" because they do not require drivers to take their eyes off the road or their hands off the steering wheel. However, as we shall see, a driver can be looking ahead but still be distracted if his or her mind is elsewhere. In practice, the riskiness of a distraction depends on a number of factors: how distracting the activity is, how often you do it, how long it takes and when it is done. Thus you could argue that selecting a radio station might be highly distracting because drivers take their eyes off the road and their hand off the steering wheel. However, it's probably not too risky in practice because it's done relatively infrequently, isn't mentally taxing and takes only a second or so to do, and the driver can choose when to do it. Answering a call on a mobile phone will be riskier, because it involves an extended period of distraction, it's often mentally demanding and – if the driver is receiving a call – the driver has little control over when the call occurs.

Research has shown that drivers are distracted more often than you might expect. In the United States, the Virginia Tech Transportation Institute has conducted a number of naturalistic studies of driving behaviour. They equip volunteers' cars with a multitude of small cameras to record what's happening inside and outside the vehicle. They also install forward radar, alcohol sensors, accelerometers and GPS. The volunteers are then left to drive around as they would normally. Because accidents are relatively rare events, most studies of this kind have been too small scale for any firm conclusions to be drawn about collisions and the events leading up to them. However, Virginia Tech's latest study, published in 2016, monitored over 3,500 drivers during a three-year period and recorded data from over 35 million miles of driving. This is enough to capture a sizeable sample of accidents and look at the events leading up to them.

Tom Dingus and his group of researchers were able to look at 905 crashes involving injury and/or property damage. Their study used a "case-control" technique: they looked at what drivers were doing immediately before a crash and compared this to a large baseline sample of events that did not lead to a crash. This enabled the researchers to calculate odds ratios – how much more likely a driver is to crash if he or she is engaged in a particular behaviour, compared to if he or she is being a "model driver" (alert, attentive and sober).

Overall, drivers were engaged in distracting activities for more than half of the time they drove, doubling their risk of crashing compared to when they were undistracted. However, the category of "distractions" covered a large variety of activities: eating, drinking, smoking, adjusting the vehicle controls, talking to passengers, phoning, texting and so on. Different distractions were associated with different levels of risk. Drivers were about five times more likely to crash when they were using a touchscreen than when they were undistracted. They were about four times more likely to crash if they were using a handheld mobile phone – which, interestingly, is very similar to the findings of an early study of mobile-phone-using drivers by Redelmeier and Tibshirani (1997). Dingus et al.'s study also showed that drivers were using their phone about 6% of the time. On the basis of their figures, Dingus and his colleagues concluded that 4 million of the 11 million crashes that occur annually in the United States might be avoided if drivers were not distracted.

MOBILE PHONES

The distraction that has received the most attention from psychologists has been the mobile phone. How safe is it to drive and talk on a phone at the same time? Many governments have banned drivers from using handheld phones but allowed the use of hands-free phones. As mentioned earlier, this stance is based on the assumption that drivers are safe if they have both hands on the wheel and their eyes on the road. However there is now a huge amount of evidence that drivers talking on a phone are significantly impaired, regardless of whether the phone is handheld or hands-free.

This has been demonstrated using a wide variety of techniques. Many laboratory studies use tasks similar to those in the hazard perception component of the UK driving test: participants watch video clips filmed from a driver's perspective and look for hazards. Whenever they see a hazard, they respond as quickly as they can, by pressing a button or a "brake pedal". Other studies have measured performance in driving simulators, recording how well drivers can control the vehicle (in terms of following distance, lane-keeping and so on) and how well they can respond to events such as a pedestrian stepping into the road or the vehicle in front braking suddenly. Some researchers have looked at real-world driving in instrumented cars, on closed test-tracks or even on public roads. A number of studies have investigated how drivers' eye movements are affected by phone-use and some have used EEG equipment to examine the effects of phone-use on brain activity.

There can be few areas of psychology in which the results are so consistent. Atchley, Tran and Salehinejad (2017) aggregated the data from 342 studies on driver distraction. With respect to the effects of mobile-phone-use, the picture that emerged was very clear: of 147 performance measurements that were made, 82% showed evidence of impairment when a handheld phone was being used. This was strikingly similar to the effects of hands-free phones, where 81% of 270 measurements showed impairment.

Lane-keeping and following distance (headway) tend to become more inconsistent when drivers are using a phone. These measures were the focus of early studies, largely because these aspects of driving performance are easy to quantify. However, from the point of view of road safety, the most important effects of phone-use are the *cognitive* impairments. Many studies have now demonstrated that phone-using drivers notice fewer hazards and they take longer to react to the ones that they do detect. Response times in an emergency braking situation are *at least* half a second longer than when the driver is undistracted. (Many studies show much greater increases, so this is a very conservative estimate.) Half a second might not sound like much, but at 113 kilometres per hour (70 miles per hour), a car is travelling at 31 metres (101.7 feet) *per second*. A phone-using driver on a motorway will be adding 15 metres to the normal braking distance. That's the length of about four Ford Fiestas. Half a second can easily be the difference between hitting something and avoiding a collision altogether, or the difference between a survivable collision and a fatal one.

The eye-tracking studies show that phone-use affects drivers' scanning patterns; they tend to stare straight ahead, in the direction of travel and look much less to the sides of the vehicle or behind. Drivers are also much less responsive to events occurring in those regions, so that they demonstrate a kind of "cognitive tunnel vision". Drivers can be unresponsive to events occurring in front of them too: eye-tracking studies show that they can fail to respond to potential hazards even though their eyes are fixated directly upon the hazard. (Recall the discussion of "looked but failed to see" accidents in Chapter 1).

In Chapter 1, I mentioned "Inattentional Blindness": if you are preoccupied with performing one visual task, you may be entirely unaware of changes that are unrelated to that task, even if they occur in the same region of space. A good demonstration of how using a phone produces Inattentional Blindness comes from a study by Hyman et al. (2010). They filmed pedestrians walking across a courtyard and recorded whether they were walking alone and undistracted, walking with a friend, using an MP3 music player or using their mobile phone. The phone-users bumped into other people more often. There was a unicycling clown in the courtyard. When accosted as they left the square and asked if they saw anything unusual, only 25% of the phone-users reported seeing the clown, as opposed to 61% of the MP3 users.

All of these effects on drivers' performance can be summed up as representing problems with "Situation Awareness". In the context of driving, having good Situation Awareness means you are fully aware of what other road-users are doing now and what they are likely to do in the near future. Most of the impairments shown by phone-using drivers can be seen as symptoms of an underlying deficit in Situation Awareness. Their "eye freezing" means that they are unlikely to obtain information about anything other than the region immediately ahead of their vehicle, and if they are concentrating on their "inner world", even information from this region may not receive much attention. Phone-using drivers use their mirrors less, so they won't know what is going on behind them. Because they are less aware of their surroundings, they are unable to anticipate emerging hazards and less able to cope with unexpected events.

Finally, there is some evidence from EEG studies that a mobile phone conversation can be distracting even after it has finished. Rumination (mulling over the contents of the conversation) impairs hazard detection performance and produces EEG changes reflecting reduced activation in visual areas of the brain and increased activity in areas involved in problem-solving. This may account for a curious finding noted by Redelmeier and Tibshirani (1997) in their study of real-world drivers twenty years ago: mobile-phone-using drivers were at increased risk of an accident not just during the conversation but for ten minutes afterwards.

David Strayer and his colleagues at the University of Utah have compared mobile-phone-use to other potential distractors (review in Strayer, Watson and Drews, 2011). Using a simulator, they found that a mobile phone conversation was more disruptive to drivers' performance than merely listening to a radio play. Passively listening to the radio taxes mental resources much less than a conversation because talking to someone is *interactive*: drivers have to decode what the other person is saying, remember it and think of what they are going to say themselves. A conversation may well involve problem-solving of some kind, which additionally uses up mental resources.

All of these things apply as much to a conversation with a passenger inside the vehicle as to a mobile phone conversation. However, mobile phone conversations are more distracting than conversations with passengers, as demonstrated by studies showing that blindfolded car passengers are more distracting than passengers who can see. Firstly, sighted passengers are aware of the driver's current situation; they can see the state of the traffic for themselves and assess whether the driver is likely to be able to cope with talking and driving at the same time. They can therefore adjust their conversation to suit, perhaps pausing the conversation while the driver emerges from a tricky junction or negotiates a roundabout. Someone on the other end of a phone cannot do this. Secondly, face-to-face conversation employs lots of subtle non-verbal cues that facilitate turn-taking. Maintaining a conversation with someone you cannot see has to be achieved without these aids and is therefore much harder work mentally.

THEORETICAL MODELS OF ATTENTION AND DUAL-TASKING

It is clear that using a mobile phone impairs driving performance, but why does it do so? After all, under some circumstances, we *do* appear to be able to multi-task quite effectively. My favourite example is the 19th-century composer and virtuoso pianist Franz Liszt. He practiced scales and arpeggios for hours while reading a book. So why can't drivers use a phone and drive at the same time? To answer this question, we need to consider theoretical models of dual-tasking performance.

A central idea in cognitive psychology is that we have limited mental resources to use on any particular task or set of tasks. Most modern theories of attention and performance suggest that we can divide these resources amongst different activities to some extent. A popular idea is that information-processing occurs at a number of different levels, some conscious and some unconscious. Norman and Shallice's (1986) model of information-processing suggests there are two different ways in which we control our behaviour: a lower level "contention scheduling" system that is automatic and fast but fairly inflexible and a higher level "supervisory attentional system" that is slower and flexible but requires conscious information-processing (and hence takes up much of our limited cognitive resources). Environmental triggers activate schemas, patterns of behaviour that are "run off" in a fairly automatic, reflexive way. If there are competing schemas, the contention scheduling system decides which one will be executed. Much of our routine activity can be handled this way. However, in an unusual or complicated situation, the supervisory attentional system can intervene and take control of behaviour.

This model accounts for how experienced drivers can even contemplate trying to do two tasks at once; much of everyday driving is very routine and predictable, especially on familiar roads and so it can be handled by the contention scheduling system, leaving the supervisory attentional system free to deal with a phone conversation. Vehicle control (gear-changing, steering and braking) is fairly automatic and even things like choice of lane and speed often require very little conscious control. Many drivers have had the unsettling experience of arriving at some point on a familiar route and suddenly realising they have no recollection of how they got there – the so-called "driving without awareness mode" (see Chapter 6). If something unusual happens, such as a pedestrian stepping into the road ahead, then the supervisory attentional system takes over.

Norman and Shallice's model explains how drivers can manage to use a phone when driving conditions are undemanding and why they fail to cope when the conditions suddenly change and an emergency response is required. However, this model does not do justice to the fact that "driving" is not really a single task. Jens Rasmussen, a highly influential Danish human factors theorist, suggested that driving can be thought of as being organised on three levels. The lowest level is vehicle control (steering, gear-changing, braking and so on). The next level is "tactical" and involves attending to signs, pedestrians and other vehicles. The highest, "strategic" level involves processes such as choice of route, departure time and speed. While it might be possible to achieve vehicle control on the basis of contention scheduling, the higher levels of driving will require at least some degree of conscious control. Consequently interference between driving and phone-use, even in non-emergency situations, is probably greater than one might predict on the basis of a simple-minded application of Norman and Shallice's model to the question of whether drivers can multi-task.

Christopher Wickens' Multiple Resource Theory of information-processing takes a finer-grain approach to resource allocation in multi-tasking situations, to try to specify more precisely the conditions under which tasks will or will not conflict. Wickens suggests there are three dimensions that need to be considered with respect to resources: the sensory modality by which information is input (e.g., auditory, visual or tactile); the way in which the information is "coded" (e.g., either spatially or verbally); and the type of response required (e.g., manual or vocal). Tasks will interfere with each other if they compete for the same resources on any of these dimensions.

At first sight, it looks like Multiple Resource Theory would predict that driving and mobile-phone-use are compatible tasks. It could be argued that driving involves visual input, a spatial code and manual output, whereas a mobile phone conversation involves auditory input, a verbal code and a vocal output. The resources for the two tasks should be quite different on all three dimensions and so they should not interfere with each other. However, research suggests that using a mobile phone is actually a more spatial and visual task than one might at first imagine. This is because phone conversations often involve visual imagery. Imagery and "real world" perception share brain regions and hence compete directly for the same processing resources. Briggs, Hole and Land (2016) compared the effects on hazard detection of conversations which required the use of visual imagery and conversations which did not. Both types of conversation increased the amount of time that it took participants to detect hazards, but these effects were worse for the imagery-inducing conversation. Phone-using drivers may sometimes be paying more attention to their inner, imaginary visual world than the real world outside the car. As a result, they will be more likely to miss events that they should be attending to, such as emerging hazards.

Once you appreciate the true nature of the phone-using task, it is clear that Multiple Resource Theory predicts that driving and phone-use will compete for the same resources (visual input) and so interfere with each other. It also accounts for how Liszt could play and read at the same time. Practicing scales involves auditory input (hitting the right notes), a spatial code and a manual output. Reading involves a visual input, verbal code and little in the way of a manual response other than to occasionally turn the page.

It should also be noted that in Liszt's case, one of the tasks (practicing scales) was very highly practiced and highly predictable, to the point where it could be accomplished automatically. In contrast, both driving and using a mobile phone are complicated tasks which are inherently variable in nature and hence much harder to combine effectively.

WHY DO DRIVERS USE MOBILE PHONES?

If mobile-phone-use affects performance so badly, why do drivers do it? Phone-use remains widespread, despite publicity campaigns warning of the dangers and media coverage of fatal accidents caused by drivers on mobile phones.

The Theory of Planned Behaviour suggests that the likelihood of someone engaging in a behaviour is determined by its benefits, costs and acceptability. For many drivers, using a mobile phone has strong immediate benefits, such as avoiding boredom, greater work efficiency and maintaining social contact with friends and family. It has low perceived costs, since drivers believe there is little or no risk of an accident occurring while they are using the phone and only a very slim chance of being caught by the police if they use a handheld phone. Phone-use while driving is a highly acceptable behaviour for many drivers and their peers.

Interestingly, a number of surveys have shown that many drivers admit to using a phone while driving, despite noticing that other drivers are impaired by using their phone! There are probably a number of psychological factors behind this logical inconsistency. People often show "self-serving bias": they have an inflated view of their own abilities (and luck!) compared to other people's, so they believe that *other* drivers are impaired but that *they* can cope with using a phone while driving. As we shall see in Chapter 5, people's assessment of risk is quite irrational; they think they have more control over the driving situation than they actually do and they have "protective beliefs" (such as "I use a phone, but I'm safe because I only do so when the roads are quiet" or "I leave more room between me and the vehicle in front to compensate for my slower reactions when I'm on the phone"). Zhou, Yu and Wang (2016) showed that having these protective beliefs was very common amongst mobile-phone-using drivers and indeed was a significant *predictor* of their readiness to use a mobile phone: drivers who held more of these beliefs were more likely to make a phone call or send a text whilst driving. (Phone-using drivers often do attempt to make some allowance for their impairment, by driving more slowly and leaving a bigger gap between their vehicle and the one in front. However because the drivers underestimate how impaired they actually are, these increased safety margins are inadequate compensation).

Drivers' misperceptions of risk are compounded by the fact that accidents are rare, so there are usually no immediate penalties for using the phone while driving. Every trip without an accident reinforces the driver's delusion that using a phone is "safe". Because they are distracted by the conversation, phone-using drivers lack Situation Awareness. Driving is fairly predictable and so compensating for reduced Situation Awareness by falling back on well-established schemas will often suffice. However, the drivers fail to notice their own impairment (including the unexpected hazards that they are failing to detect) or the actions of other drivers that may compensate for their poor driving. Hence, they receive little feedback about their poor driving, except when an accident actually occurs.

As we shall see in Chapter 3, many drivers think being a good driver is synonymous with having good vehicle control skills, rather than good hazard perception abilities, so if they monitor their own driving at all, they find little or no impairment in their steering and lane-keeping and therefore conclude that their driving is unimpaired. And, of course, governments' inconsistent policies with respect to the legality of mobile-phone-use mean that many drivers are misled into believing that hands-free phones are "safe".

TEXTING

Surely the ultimate distraction while driving is to read or write text messages – and yet this behaviour is widespread. Surveys suggest that overall, around 30% of drivers admit to at least occasionally sending or reading a text while driving. But this figure is around 50 to 70% for young drivers, which is particularly worrying given the under-25s are the age group who are most at risk of having an accident anyway (see Chapter 3). Again, the Theory of Planned Behaviour can explain why drivers engage in this idiotic activity: the benefits of being in social contact are perceived as high; the costs (risk of accident or prosecution) are perceived as low; and, amongst young drivers at least, texting is seen as a socially acceptable thing to do.

As with mobile phones, drivers try to ameliorate the risks by texting only when stationary, such as at traffic lights, or when they perceive the road conditions to be "safe". However, even texting at traffic lights is risky because of the mental overheads produced by rumination. Also, it's quite likely that the text will not be completed before the lights change. Consequently, drivers have to remember where they were in the process of writing the text, remember what they want to text, and remember that they need to finish the text at the next available opportunity. Given that the text is likely to be part of an extended interchange, which introduces additional demands on memory, the potential for distraction is clear.

A recent survey of research on texting by Jeff Caird and his co-workers concluded that sending or reading texts significantly disrupted almost every aspect of driving performance. Research on hands-free speech-based interfaces suggests that they are no solution. Although the primary impairments produced by texting are the obvious ones (diversion of attention away from the external world and impaired vehicle control), texting also has cognitive effects, in terms of mental distraction and an increase in mental workload, and these are not ameliorated by "hands-free" interfaces.

CONCLUSION

Human beings are naturally distractible. In our evolutionary past, it was beneficial not to become too preoccupied with a task and to remain alert for possible predators, enemies and the like. Being distracted during driving is almost inevitable; it would be unrealistic to expect drivers to be totally focused on driving 100% of the time. However, self-inflicted distraction for prolonged periods during driving, as a consequence of phoning or texting, is another matter.

How distraction translates into an increased risk of an accident is hard to determine (although studies of naturalistic driving like Dingus et al.'s give us some idea). However a huge amount of research now shows that using a phone (let alone texting) measurably impairs drivers' performance. This is true regardless of whether the phone is handheld or hands-free. In terms of the level of distraction, phone conversations are not the same as talking to someone within the vehicle. To make matters worse, it is the very age group that are at most risk of an accident in the first place (the under-25-year-olds) who are most likely to phone or text while driving.

Most of the time, drivers appear to manage to combine mobile-phone-use and driving without crashing. One explanation for this may lie in Stanton et al.'s (2006) concept of Distributed Situation Awareness. Earlier in this chapter, we considered SA from the viewpoint of the individual driver, but you could think of it being "distributed", shared amongst drivers in a given locale. This makes for a forgiving system: if one driver has reduced SA because he or she is distracted, then other drivers with fuller SA can compensate for this, so there are no adverse consequences. In short, other drivers can make allowances for the distracted driver's poor driving. Accidents will only occur when the distributed SA cannot cope with the situation – for example, when someone steps off the pavement unexpectedly. Here, everything depends on the SA of the individual driver nearest the event, and if that driver happens to be distracted by a phone conversation, an accident is likely to happen.

The root problem stems from the fact that driving is, as Hancock, Lesch and Simmons (2003) memorably put it, "long periods of sub-critical demand interspersed with moments of crucial response, or hours of boredom interspersed with moments of terror". The driving environment is relatively forgiving, because there is a lot of predictability in the system and other drivers compensate for the distracted driver's impairments. Consequently, most of the time, the distracted driver manages to cope. The problem comes when something unexpected happens that requires an emergency response. It is then that the dual-tasking driver finds him- or herself critically under-equipped to deal with the situation.

3

DRIVING, RISK AND YOUTH

INTRODUCTION

Many people would be reluctant to stand near the edge of a high cliff with a sheer drop that would certainly kill them if they took a few steps forwards. However, most of us are quite comfortable driving along a high-speed road, with the oncoming traffic only a couple of feet away. Why are we generally so unconcerned about the risks of driving compared to other activities? How do we assess the risks of driving, and why do some people drive more riskily than others?

THEORIES OF RISK PERCEPTION

Explanations of how people assess the riskiness of their driving have been largely dominated by the idea of "risk compensation". It's suggested that drivers adjust their behaviour to maintain a certain preferred level of risk. If driving is made safer, drivers will behave more riskily to compensate and vice versa. (When people discover what I do for a living, they will often tell me that everyone would drive more safely if there was a ten-inch spike attached to the centre of the steering wheel. As we'll see, they probably wouldn't.)

Gerald Wilde's Risk Homoeostasis Theory proposes that we each have a preferred "target level" of risk, which we maintain by adjusting

our behaviour. Controversially, Wilde claims that many safety measures, such as anti-lock brakes, are doomed to fail as a result of RHT.
If drivers feel safer, they will drive more riskily, and accident rates will
remain unchanged. Wilde argues that the best way to increase road
safety is to provide incentives for people to change their target level
of risk: they have to want to drive more safely.

Drivers do seem to show some degree of risk compensation (for
example, increasing their headway while they use a mobile phone –
see Chapter 2), but Risk Homeostasis Theory is unlikely to be correct
because it is at odds with what we know about the psychology of
risk-taking and decision-making. A fundamental assumption behind
the theory is that individuals can accurately estimate the level of risk
to which they are exposed, but there's actually lots of evidence that
people are quite poor at judging risk.

Firstly, it is unlikely that drivers could get detailed feedback about
the riskiness of their behaviour. Many risky behaviours (such as overtaking on blind bends) may be performed for a long time without any
penalty and hence without the driver being able to get an accurate
idea of how dangerous they really are. Secondly, people's level of risk
is not something which is wholly under their control, because they
can be an innocent victim in an accident. Thirdly, for drivers to be
able to make accurate estimates of the risks to which they are exposed,
they would need to have a good memory for what has happened to
them, in terms of near-misses and accidents. In fact, drivers' memories of their accident records (and hence their ability to estimate
how much risk they are being exposed to) are highly fallible (see
Chapter 5 on personality).

The most compelling evidence against RHT comes from psychological studies of decision-making. These suggest that people are very
poor at making rational estimates of the likelihood of events. A series
of highly influential studies by Tversky and Kahneman (1973) showed
that humans often use various "heuristics" as a basis for their actions,
rough-and-ready "rules of thumb" that can provide an answer to a
problem fairly easily and quickly but not always very accurately.

One of these is the "availability" heuristic: reasoning is affected by how easily relevant information comes to mind. This leads people astray when it comes to evaluating the likelihood of having an accident. Many people have a seriously distorted view of the relative safety of air, train and car travel. Because airplane crashes are very rare, they attract a lot of media attention when they do occur. This makes the possibility of an air disaster much more salient to people and leads them to seriously overestimate the risk of being in a plane crash themselves.

A final problem for RHT is that drivers tend to suffer from an over-inflated opinion of their own abilities. Surveys have often found that *most* drivers consider themselves to be more skilful and safer than the average driver. Why do many drivers think they are better than average? One reason is that people tend to look more favourably upon their own actions than those of others. Consequently, they see their mistakes as less important or more justifiable than those of other people. Attribution theory states that people tend to explain their own behaviour as being due to the situation in which they find themselves, whereas the behaviour of other people is attributed to those people's own stable personal traits. Therefore, a driver's own mistakes are attributed to the situation (e.g., "I missed that red light because the bright sunlight made it hard to see"), but other drivers make mistakes because they possess the trait of being a "bad driver" ("he drove through that red light because he is reckless or inattentive").

One reason for drivers having a distorted idea of their own abilities is that after passing their test, they rarely get any independent evaluation of their driving. Duncan, Williams and Brown (1991) found that experience *per se* did not necessarily lead to the development of driving expertise. For scanning, anticipation and safety margins, experienced drivers (i.e., drivers who had merely been driving a long time) were actually poorer than novices. Similar conclusions can be drawn from a study by Amado et al. (2014). They compared drivers' evaluations of their own driving during an 80-minute on-road session to assessments by an expert observer. Ninety-five percent of the drivers overestimated every aspect of their driving competence, compared to what the expert thought. This was especially so for drivers whom the expert rated as "unsafe". The discrepancy between the expert's ratings and the drivers' self-assessments increased as the drivers' experience increased, suggesting that experience did not lead drivers to develop better self-insight.

Drivers' distorted opinions of their own skills may lead them to underestimate how much they are at risk of an accident. It may also affect their perception of accident statistics, reinforcing their belief that an accident is something that happens to other people (i.e., less competent drivers). The fact that they haven't had an accident (yet) is attributed to their own skill, rather than to luck.

Finally, let's return to that idea about making drivers safer by putting a spike on the steering wheel. Research shows that people who are behaving riskily do *not* compensate for their increased riskiness in other ways. For example, drivers who do not use seatbelts tend to be young, male and more likely to drive riskily – in other words, members of the very group of drivers who are mostly likely to crash. They have higher rates of accidents and violations, consume more drugs and alcohol and are more likely to use handheld mobile phones (a behaviour which increases the risk of an accident – see Chapter 4).

All these studies suggest that the drivers who are most likely to have an accident are the ones who are *least* likely to try to compensate for their increased risk. There are two ways in which RHT could try to explain these findings. One is to suggest that risky drivers are prepared to accept much higher target levels of risk than other drivers, which seems implausible. Alternatively, it could be argued that perhaps risky drivers misperceive the riskiness of their behaviour; they strive to maintain a similar level of target risk to everyone else but seriously underestimate the objective risk to which they are actually exposed. Lesch and Hancock (2004) have shown that, for female drivers at least, drivers' confidence in their ability to cope with using a mobile phone while driving bears no relation to their actual driving performance. Thus, drivers may underestimate the riskiness of their behaviour because they overestimate their own competence.

Brown and Cotton (2003) provide evidence that drivers who speed may hold "risk-mitigating" beliefs which cause them to underestimate the true risks associated with speeding. For example, compared to drivers who do not speed, they are more likely to agree with statements such as "I can drive safely at speed" and "only really high speeds are dangerous". These beliefs are erroneous, in the sense that they are contradicted by the accident statistics. Brown and Cotton suggest that speeding drivers may be in a state of self-deception, similar to that of smokers who convince themselves that exercise will reduce their risks of contracting lung disease. The important point, for the current argument, is that this is yet another demonstration of people's irrationality in judging risk.

To sum up, everything we know about the psychology of risk perception suggests it is highly unlikely that people could evaluate risk levels accurately enough for RHT to work. People are actually very poor at assessing the riskiness of their activities; risk assessment is irrational and prone to bias from many extraneous factors.

Alternative explanations of driver behaviour include the idea that there is effectively no "risk perception" at all, because drivers do not feel as if they are engaging in a risky behaviour. Although driving is probably the riskiest activity that most people engage in, it's still very safe in absolute terms. In 2016, out of the 581,776 people who died in the UK, only 1,792 of them did so in road accidents. There were 37 million licensed vehicles in the UK that year.

Heikki Summala's "zero-risk" theory of driving proposes that drivers seldom think about risks at all. Instead, they control risk primarily by maintaining safety margins around themselves. For example, they have an area of space around the car which is kept free of other road-users, and they maintain a satisfactory time-to-collision between themselves and other vehicles. These behaviours are largely habitual and automatic.

Summala suggests accidents occur because drivers underestimate the actual risks of driving. Firstly, they fail to take account of the variability in the traffic system. Thus, they might fail to allow for the fact that the person in front might have to brake suddenly or that another driver might change lanes without warning. Secondly, drivers' safety margins are often inadequate because they drive too fast. Drivers overestimate the usefulness of speed as a means to get to their destination quicker; they are reluctant to reduce speed, and they use speed to impress others.

Ultimately, there is the same problem with Summala's theory as with Wilde's: although it is useful as a conceptualisation of why drivers choose the risks they do, it cannot tell us who is going to take risks, when and for precisely what reasons. For that, we need to look at the high-risk groups of drivers and try to see what differentiates them from their low-risk peers.

DIFFERENT TYPES OF RISKINESS

One limitation of risk perception theories is they fail to acknowledge that apparently "risky" behaviours can occur for reasons other than calculated riskiness on the part of a driver. On the basis of responses to their "Driver Behaviour Questionnaire", James Reason and his colleagues suggested that aberrant behaviours by drivers could be divided into three types: "errors" (behaviours which are inappropriate for the situation, such as failing to notice a "Give Way" sign or turning right when one meant to turn left); "slips" and "lapses" (unintended omissions of actions, such as forgetting to cancel an indicator); and "violations" (deliberate flouting of traffic laws or safe practices, such as running a red light).

Overall, in Reason et al.'s original study and in subsequent replications, women report making more errors than men, but men report committing more violations. The three types of aberrant behaviour also show different age patterns; with increasing age, drivers make fewer violations and more lapses. Errors don't change with age. For violations, social and motivational factors seem to be important, whereas errors are claimed to represent information-processing failures. The participants who reported the most violations rated themselves as particularly skilful drivers; they appeared to believe that a good driver is someone who can bend the rules. However, research actually shows that accidents are linked to the propensity to commit violations, rather than a tendency to make errors. Young male drivers, the demographic group who are at most risk of an accident, commit the most violations.

THE "YOUNG DRIVER" PROBLEM

Accident statistics show clearly that the risk of an accident varies considerably depending on the driver's age and gender. Younger drivers (under 25 years of age) are most at risk, especially if they are male. In the UK, about a quarter of drivers in this age group have an accident within two years of passing their driving test. Worldwide, road accidents are the single biggest cause of death for young adults (WHO 2015).

As age increases, the accident rate declines, so that middle-aged drivers (40- to 50-year-olds) have the lowest accident rates. Accident risk rises again in old age (75 years plus) but not to the level of the young drivers. Women show a similar age pattern to men but have fewer accidents than men at all ages (about half as many).

Why are young drivers, especially males, so much more at risk of an accident than older drivers? It's rather paradoxical when you consider that young drivers generally have the best eyesight, the fastest reaction times and possibly the best vehicle control skills. These are all characteristics that many drivers (especially young ones!) would say are important for good driving.

Limited driving experience

The most obvious reason is that young drivers have only limited driving experience. One problem is that young drivers' vehicle control skills develop faster than their hazard perception abilities. The result is novice drivers who can drive fast but who fail to appreciate that their speed is dangerous because they are unaware of the hazards around them. Research suggests that drivers, especially young males, erroneously equate safety with high levels of skill in vehicle control.

In reality, safe driving is correlated with good hazard perception, not control skills. In fact, one study found that racing drivers had *more* accidents when they drove on public roads than did a group of normal drivers.

Psychosocial benefits of risky driving

Inexperience can't be the whole explanation, because otherwise young men and women would have similar accident rates. And not *all* young drivers have accidents; some are riskier than others. There must be other factors at play. One is the way in which young male drivers use driving as a tool for increasing their prestige amongst their peers. Researchers are coming to appreciate that risky driving can have *benefits* for young drivers, rather than merely being dysfunctional behaviour.

Australian psychologists Bridie Scott-Parker, Mark King and Barry Watson suggest that young drivers often drive merely for "psycho-social" reasons rather than to get to a particular destination. Young males are more likely to report driving to gain status with their peers, to feel powerful and to relax. Females are more likely to drive in order to obtain a sense of freedom and independence. Drivers who report driving to gain social status and spend time with their friends seem to be more likely to engage in risky driving (speeding and tailgating). Teenage drivers are more likely to have an accident if they have other teenagers (i.e., their friends) as passengers in the car. This risk factor is acknowledged in the "graduated licence" schemes that have been introduced in some countries; these often ban young drivers from taking passengers, especially at night.

You get it from your family

Taubman-Ben-Ari and his colleagues have long been interested in the influence of friends and family on young drivers' behaviour. Their research is consistent with previous work suggesting that parents can influence the riskiness of their children's driving in several ways. The quality of the parent-child relationship is important: young drivers who report emotional detachment from their family, or an inability to achieve independence and autonomy, tend to report that they drive more riskily and have more crashes than other young drivers. Safer young drivers tend to report that their parents monitor their driving behaviour, laying down clear rules about the circumstances under which they can use the car and about unsafe behaviours, such as using a mobile phone or not using a seatbelt. Parental standards are not just communicated directly but also by how the parents themselves drive: in the context of driving, parents act as important role models for their children.

Taubman-Ben-Ari has long advocated the development of "holistic" models of driver behaviour, envisaging reckless driving behaviour as the net outcome of both personal characteristics and the young driver's perception and interpretation of various environmental influences, such as friends and family. Young male drivers are likely to see risky driving as a challenge, overestimate their ability to cope, disregard its possible outcomes (either through ignorance or a misplaced sense of invulnerability), and be unduly influenced by unsafe role models.

CONCLUSION

Despite its intuitive plausibility, there's little evidence that drivers' riskiness is determined by any process of "risk compensation". Everything we know about the psychology of human reasoning suggests that people's estimates of the risks of driving are heavily influenced by irrational factors, such as the availability heuristic and the extent to which drivers feel they have control over the risk. Drivers' assessment of the riskiness of their own behaviour is likely to be distorted by a host of false beliefs, stemming from self-serving bias ("I'm better than other drivers"), optimism bias ("accidents happen to other people, not to me") and protective beliefs ("I can speed because it's late at night and there's no one around").

Probably the biggest problem is that most drivers simply do not perceive driving as particularly risky. Because road accidents are so commonplace they do not warrant media attention unless they are particularly spectacular or tragic. Consequently, the riskiness of driving is unlikely to be uppermost in people's minds. Also, road accidents are spread amongst 37 million licensed drivers, so any particular individual driver is unlikely to be involved in a serious accident on any given journey. This is a problem for safety campaigns: telling drivers to stop speeding or texting because these behaviours are dangerous simply does not square with their everyday experiences. Every trip completed without an accident reinforces risky drivers in the delusion that they are "safe" and that accidents happen to someone else, not them. Coupled with self-serving bias and drivers' inflated ideas of their own competence, it is unsurprising that road safety campaigns have been found to be rather ineffective at changing drivers' behaviour.

One very clear finding is that young male drivers are most at risk of an accident. Their risky behaviour arises from the interaction of numerous factors, including a predisposition to thrill-seeking, poor hazard perception, an inflated idea of their own abilities and a desire to impress their peers. Let's take the example of speeding. The Theory of Planned Behaviour states that behaviour is best predicted from people's intentions. Intentions depend on three things: the person's attitude to the behaviour, subjective norms and the extent to which the person perceives he or she has control over his or her behaviour. Young drivers may have a positive attitude to speeding: it's exciting, they are unaware of its possible adverse consequences (because of their inexperience) and it gives them prestige because they think it will impress their passengers. Their subjective norm is that speeding is socially acceptable: everyone does it, it's often extolled as a virtue in the media and their friends and family don't disapprove of it. Finally, young drivers perceive speeding as something they have little control over; it would be hard to resist speeding because their friends would think less of them if they drove in a boringly "safe" way.

Novice drivers are likely to engage in a constellation of risky behaviours (driving too fast for the conditions, under the influence of drugs and alcohol or without a seatbelt) that make them both more likely to have an accident and also less likely to survive it. Effective interventions to reduce their riskiness require an appreciation of how all these factors interact. They are unlikely to succeed unless they take account of the psychological *value* of risky driving for young drivers, in terms of how it affects their self-esteem, feelings of independence and prestige in the eyes of their friends.

4

THE EFFECTS OF AGE ON DRIVING

HOW RISKY ARE OLDER DRIVERS?

Type "elderly driver" into Google, and you will find innumerable complaints about the dangers posed by elderly drivers. They are claimed to have dangerously poor eyesight and excessively long reaction times, and it's alleged that they cause lots of accidents because of their enfeebled cognitive capacity and general incompetence at driving. These rants are usually bolstered by references to the occasional highly publicised case of an elderly driver doing something dangerous, such as driving the wrong way up a motorway. The proposed "remedy" is to introduce compulsory eyesight tests and maybe even medicals for every driver over the age of 65 (or whatever age the writer regards as "old").

Some elderly drivers undoubtedly do experience difficulties whilst driving, but many do not. As we shall see, these negative stereotypes are quite at odds with the scientific evidence on elderly drivers as a group. However, the safety of elderly drivers does need to be evaluated, because most developed countries will show a marked increase in the proportion of elderly drivers over the next few decades. In the UK, in 1975, only 30% of men and 5% of women aged over 70 had a driving licence. By 2014, this had risen to 80% of men and 50% of women. In 2016, 4.5 million people aged 70 or above held driving licences (including 236 centenarians!). This number is likely to double within the next 20 years. If there is any problem with elderly drivers, it is likely to get worse as numbers increase.

Conversely, it is equally important to maintain elderly people's access to personal transport for as long as possible. In contrast to previous generations, the elderly people of today have grown up with a car and are often heavily reliant on it. Research suggests that the social isolation which elderly people often experience after giving up their car can lead to depression and accelerated health decline.

STATISTICAL ANALYSES OF THE EFFECTS OF AGE ON RISKINESS

Let's begin with looking at the accident statistics. Most countries show a similar U-shaped pattern, with accidents more common amongst very young and very old drivers than amongst middle-aged ones. In 2014, a multidisciplinary group called the Older Drivers Task Force produced a report summarising the evidence on the riskiness of elderly drivers in the UK (Road Safety Foundation, n.d.). Figure 5.5 shows the casualty rates for different age groups, taking into account the severity of the injuries incurred (from slight injury through to fatal accidents).

In line with many other studies, the accident rate is highest by far for young drivers and then steeply declines with age. Drivers aged between 30 and 65 are the safest. The casualty rates then rise again to some degree. However, it's important to note that the extent of the rise in old age depends on which measure you look at. For accidents involving slight injuries, it increases only a little, but for fatal injuries, it rises steeply from about 75 years of age onwards. This is mainly because older people are much less likely to survive an accident than younger ones. Older drivers also tend to drive small, older cars, which are less crashworthy. So, if you look solely at age changes in fatality rates, you get a distorted impression of elderly drivers' riskiness. Rather than simply jump to the conclusion that elderly drivers show an elevated death rate because of the way they drive, we need to

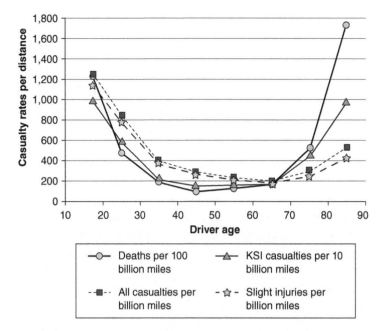

Figure 5.5 The relationship between driver age and rates of accidents of varying severity.

consider that this spike might really be an artefact produced by their greater fragility. Elderly drivers are more likely to enter the accident statistics than younger drivers, merely because they are more likely to die or be seriously hurt in any accidents in which they are involved.

There is yet another complication in interpreting the performance of elderly drivers: the issue of exposure to risk. Surveys suggest that many elderly drivers are aware their abilities are declining and try to compensate for this. They drive less often, drive shorter distances and stick to familiar roads. They avoid difficult driving conditions, such as tricky junctions, rush-hour traffic, poor weather and night-time driving. They drive more slowly and leave more distance between themselves and the vehicle in front.

How this affects their accident rates is an interesting question. Elderly drivers might be expected to have fewer accidents than younger drivers simply because they reduce their exposure to hazardous driving conditions. You might even argue that if elderly drivers are having more accidents despite this, then perhaps they are even riskier than the accident statistics suggest. However, there is another way of looking at the consequences of the elderly drivers' behavioural adaptations. The Finnish psychologist Liisa Hakamies-Blomqvist has pointed out that, regardless of age, low-mileage drivers will tend to appear less safe than high-mileage drivers. High-mileage drivers tend to spend a lot of time on high-speed roads, such as motorways, which are statistically the safest roads to travel on. Low-mileage drivers tend to spend their time on lower-speed roads. These have many more junctions at which drivers can come into conflict with each other. Thus, the accident rate per mile travelled will look worse for the low-mileage driver, for reasons that have little to do with the person's age.

So far, I've discussed overall accident rates. If we consider the elderly driver's behaviour in more detail, we continue to get a broadly positive picture. Scores of studies have shown that drivers over the age of 70 are less likely than younger drivers to be involved in accidents involving alcohol, excessive speed, overtaking, close following or loss of control of the vehicle. They are less likely to commit traffic violations than younger drivers. Tests of self-reported driver behaviour tend to show that older drivers have better attitudes towards driving than younger drivers.

However, a large number of studies have also shown that older drivers do appear to have a problem in one specific area: emerging from a junction at which they have to give way or stop, especially if they have to deal with two lanes of traffic at the same time (by turning right in the UK or left in countries which drive on the right). Lombardi, Horrey and Courtney (2017) analysed the data from 48,733 fatal intersection collisions in the United States between 2011 and 2014. Drivers over the age of 85 were almost twice as likely as younger drivers to be killed. Elderly drivers are also more likely to be at fault in junction collisions. In Lombardi et al.'s study, 56% of drivers aged over 65 were deemed responsible for their collision, compared to only 38% of drivers aged 65 or less.

Elderly drivers appear to experience particular difficulty with turns that require them to find a suitable gap in both streams of approaching traffic and then make the necessary turning manoeuvre. Interestingly, very elderly women drivers are involved in more accidents than their male peers, especially at junctions. To find out why junctions are so problematic, we need to investigate the effects of ageing in greater detail.

STUDIES OF ELDERLY DRIVERS' VISUAL AND COGNITIVE ABILITIES

Eyesight

It's often asserted that elderly drivers have dangerously poor eyesight, but there's little evidence for this claim. "Static acuity" refers to sharpness of vision as measured by the ability to detect fine detail in a stationary pattern. This is usually tested with the eyechart devised by Hermann Snellen in the 19th century. The Snellen score contains two numbers: the first is the individual's performance, and the second is "normal" performance. If you have 6/6 vision, this means that you can read at 6 metres something that a normal person can read at 6 metres – i.e., you have normal visual acuity ("20/20 vision", in pre-metric units). If you have a Snellen score of 6/12, you need to be at a distance of 6 metres to be able to read what the average person can read at 12 metres. Many young people have better than "average" vision: at the age of 20, the mean is 6/4.2 (so they can read at 6 metres what the average person would need to be at 4 metres to read). In the UK, drivers must be able to read a number-plate at 20 metres (which is about 6/12).

In the past, there have been some large-scale studies investigating the relationship between static acuity and age. Davison and Irving (1980) measured the Snellen acuities of 1,400 drivers. Mean acuity at 20 years of age was better than average, at 6/4.2. Acuity decreased throughout adulthood but deteriorated sharply from the early 40s onwards. By the age of 70, it was around 6/7.3 – so nearly double that of the younger drivers but still comfortably exceeding the legal standard for driving. Less than 5% of drivers had acuity worse than 6/12, even amongst the older drivers. A study of 30,000 70-year-old Canadian drivers found that those with poor static acuity had the same risk of accidents as similarly aged drivers with better acuity.

It has been argued that other measures of eyesight are more relevant to driving, such as dynamic acuity (sensitivity to moving patterns) and contrast sensitivity (the amount of light and dark needed to detect a pattern). Again, these measures show age-related decline, but they too have little relationship to accident rates.

Attention

Perhaps elderly drivers have difficulties with allocating their attention effectively to different parts of the visual field. There is evidence that this ability declines with age, although there are large individual differences. One widely used test of divided attention is the Useful Field of View test (UFOV), devised by Karlene Ball and Cynthia Owsley (1992). It examines how well drivers can attend to stimuli presented simultaneously in their central and peripheral vision, on the assumption that safe driving requires drivers to have a broad span of attention. A typical test requires them to look at a computer screen and identify a centrally viewed target (a silhouette of a lorry or car), while having to locate a peripherally presented stimulus (a silhouette of a car), which can be at any one of a number of different locations.

Ball and Owsley found that "at fault" accident rates during a three-year period correlated better with UFOV measurements than with measures of static acuity, contrast sensitivity or mental status. Although the UFOV was the best of these tests at identifying the "unsafe" drivers in this sample, it was still relatively poor at discriminating them from perfectly safe drivers.

More recently, it's been suggested that elderly drivers' increased involvement in collisions at junctions might be due to reduced sensitivity to motion in their peripheral vision. Devised by Steven Henderson and his colleagues, the Peripheral Motion Contrast Threshold test measures how much contrast is required to detect a pattern moving in peripheral vision. Compared to young drivers, older drivers (aged 65+) needed more contrast to see the pattern, and their performance on the PMCT was moderately correlated with various measures of driving simulator performance. However, as with many of these tests, there was wide variation in performance amongst the elderly participants; many of them had performance within the range of the younger group, suggesting that age-related decline in peripheral motion processing is not an inevitable consequence of ageing.

Information-processing

Some authors have suggested that as we age, it takes us longer to perform many information-processing operations and that this decrease in processing speed is a fundamental cause of the elderly's impaired performance on many cognitive tasks – not just in terms of how quickly the tasks are carried out but also in terms of how many errors are made. These differences are very small in absolute terms, so whether they are likely to have any significant effect on driving performance remains to be determined.

Together with the attentional problems, generalised cognitive slowing might contribute to the pattern of problems shown by some elderly drivers, especially their difficulties with intersections. Because of cognitive slowing, subjectively things may happen faster to elderly drivers, since they need more time than younger drivers for each cognitive operation that they perform. To some extent, an elderly driver can compensate for any cognitive slowing by driving more slowly, cautiously and defensively. Driving is a "self-paced" activity, so elderly drivers can cope with the rapidly changing situations of normal driving reasonably well by exposing themselves to these situations at a slower rate.

In most situations, driving slowly works well, and as Hakamies-Blomqvist has pointed out, it makes the average elderly driver a comparatively safe driver. However, intersections are the one situation in which the pace of events is outside of the control of the driver.

To emerge from a busy junction, a driver needs to assess the situation rapidly, look for a safe gap in the traffic in both directions and then promptly pull out. If cognitive slowing makes each of these stages take just slightly longer, an elderly driver might experience problems.

Couple this with attentional problems, exacerbated by the fact that stress and anxiety are known to produce a narrowing of the effective field of view, and one can see why elderly drivers might be at more risk of causing collisions at intersections.

Hazard perception

While elderly drivers fare worse in laboratory tests of attention, ageing does not seem to affect their hazard perception abilities. A number of studies have shown that elderly drivers show similar scanning patterns to younger drivers, but they detect more hazards. One interpretation is that elderly drivers can operate on the basis of schemas derived from their driving experience. This enables them to anticipate hazards, largely negating the need for rapid emergency responses, whereas young drivers have to react to hazards as and when they actually occur.

AGE-RELATED ILLNESSES THAT AFFECT DRIVING

Visual pathology

As drivers age, poor vision becomes more commonplace. However, it is important to distinguish between "healthy" normal age-related deterioration and the pathological changes in eyesight due to illness which affect only a minority of drivers. Natural deterioration includes neural and retinal changes which reduce the speed at which the visual system can cope with changes in ambient illumination. These are probably the main factor in elderly drivers' reported difficulties in coping with glare from oncoming headlights. With advancing age, the lens becomes thicker, yellower and less elastic. This reduces the amount of light reaching the back of the eye, and it also causes the condition of presbyopia familiar to most people over the age of 45 or so, in which focusing on nearby objects becomes increasingly difficult. The width of the visual field (i.e., the area over which one can see) also declines somewhat with increasing age.

There are a number of pathological conditions which may impair vision enough to make driving dangerous and which are more likely to occur in the elderly. Cataracts defocus the image, producing a loss of contrast sensitivity and detail vision. Glaucoma and diabetic retinopathy damage the retina, leading to losses of peripheral vision. This may be worse for driving than loss of central vision. The normal field of view is about 200 degrees. In the UK, the legal requirement for drivers is to have a horizontal visual field of at least 120 degrees, with at least 50 degrees either side of fixation and no defects within the central 20 degrees. A series of studies by Janet Szlyk and her colleagues suggest that diseases which impair peripheral vision more than central vision are associated with higher accident rates than diseases which impair central vision more than peripheral vision (such as macular degeneration).

Strokes can produce vision loss in an entire half of the visual field (a "hemianopia") or blindness in a limited region (a "scotoma"). People are sometimes quite unaware that they have a visual field defect of this kind, especially if it covers only a relatively small area of their visual field. A survey of 10,000 drivers by Johnson and Keltner (1983) found that drivers with a significant loss of visual field in both eyes had more than double the accident rate of similarly aged drivers with intact visual fields. (Drivers with a visual field loss in one eye or who are blind in one eye seem to have similar accident rates to healthy drivers). Not all studies have found such clear effects, however, perhaps because of procedural differences in measuring visual field loss or because of individual differences in how well people cope with it.

Dementia

Although many elderly drivers appear to have some insight into their difficulties and try to restrict their driving to conditions with which they feel they can cope, there is at least one group of elderly drivers for whom this may not always be true – those in the early stages of dementia. Research suggests that most elderly people are willing to give up driving once diagnosed with dementia. However, some studies suggest that as many as 30 to 45% of people with dementia continue to drive, despite diagnosis, licence revocation and family pressure. There is also the problem that drivers can experience mild cognitive impairment (MCI) for an average of three years before they are formally identified as having Alzheimer's disease. Many of these drivers continue to drive, although they may restrict their driving to conditions they feel they can cope with.

What is the best way to identify drivers in the early stages of dementia? One approach has been to administer a test of mental competence. The most widely used of these is the Mini Mental Status Examination (MMSE). However, although performance on this test correlates with driving performance, retrospective studies have found virtually no difference between dementia patient groups that were crash free and groups that have had at least one crash.

Dobbs, Heller and Schopflocher (1998) devised a driving test that focused on the driving manoeuvres that older drivers find especially problematic, such as turns, lane changes and merging with other traffic. They tested three groups of drivers: young "normal" drivers (30 to 40 years of age), "normal" elderly drivers (aged 65 and over) and a group of similarly aged elderly drivers who were probably in the early stages of Alzheimer's disease. Sixty-eighty percent of the demented drivers, 25% of the "normal" elderly drivers and only 3% of the younger "normal" drivers failed the test. The demented group made many more hazardous errors than did the other two groups, who in turn did not differ from each other. Fifty percent of the hazardous errors were made while changing lanes, merging with other traffic or approaching intersections. Twenty-one per cent of hazardous errors occurred during left turns and 15% involved failing to stop at an intersection. The remaining errors occurred in right turns (6%) and in stopping manoeuvres (8%). Dementia affects not only cognitive abilities (visual perception, memory, concentration, problem-solving and decision-making) but also personality (producing increased aggression and disinhibition) so it's perhaps not surprising that driving is affected.

Overall, the data suggest that while the decline in driving performance due to age per se is relatively small, the impairment of elderly drivers in the early stages of dementia can be considerable. The results of Dobbs et al.'s formal testing of driving performance are in line with a number of retrospective studies which have shown that dementia sufferers are very much at risk of an accident. For example, a recent study by Lynn Meuleners and her colleagues in Australia found that a group of drivers diagnosed with dementia were almost twice as likely to have had an accident in the preceding three years (i.e., when they were probably in the early stages of dementia) compared to a similarly aged healthy group.

Marottoli and Richardson's (1998) study suggests that at least some elderly drivers lack insight about their level of impairment. Marottoli and Richardson investigated the relationship between driving performance and self-ratings of confidence and driving ability in a group of drivers aged 77 and above. All of the drivers rated themselves as being average or above-average drivers, despite the fact that nearly a third of those who were given a driving test were rated by the examiner as showing moderate or major difficulties. Drivers were also highly confident, irrespective of their level of on-road performance. As mentioned in Chapter 3, numerous researchers have shown that younger drivers overestimate their driving skills relative to their peers; it seems that this bias persists largely unchanged into late adulthood and is resistant to being changed by experiences which should provide the elderly driver with a more accurate impression of his or her abilities.

CONCLUSION

The research described in this chapter suggests that the "problem" of older drivers has been over-stated. In itself, chronological age is a poor predictor of driving ability, and many older drivers are perfectly safe. In healthy individuals, age-related declines in visual and cognitive performance are relatively small and research has consistently failed to show any strong correlations between eyesight measures, cognitive measures and accident rates.

A number of studies have looked at whether mandatory age-related re-licensing laws work in practice. Comparisons between countries or states that have such laws and similar regions that do not (for example, Finland versus Sweden, New South Wales versus Victoria, various US states) generally find that re-testing has no effect on accident rates amongst elderly drivers. There are many possible reasons for this, including the fact that re-licensing usually involves an eye test, which, as we have seen, is unlikely to identify many unsafe drivers anyway.

There is little evidence that poor visual acuity is a major factor in the increased accident risk of the elderly (or for anyone else, for that matter). This is partly because the basic capacities of the visual system are more than enough for the demands made by driving. Lane-keeping and collision-avoidance can be achieved without fine-detail vision. Many stimuli in driving merely require detection, which is an easier task than identification. For example, at a junction, one just needs to see that "something" is approaching, as opposed to identifying the make and model of the vehicle concerned. When identification is required – such as when reading road signs – the information is often well above perceptual thresholds (signs are bold, high-contrast simplified pictures designed to be easy to distinguish); it contains a degree of redundancy (e.g., signs are often repeated); and the self-paced nature of driving makes it possible for drivers to cope (e.g., they can slow down to give themselves more time to read a road sign, they can avoid driving fast at night, and so on). The importance of detection over identification explains why diseases that impair peripheral vision have more consequence for driving safety. Another factor is that much of driving is a highly predictable activity. The road environment is generally highly structured and consistent. This enables drivers to act on the basis of what they expect to encounter, rather than have to perform a detailed visual analysis of everything around them.

In recent years, research has shifted towards examining the effectiveness of test batteries that include Useful Field of View tests and

assessments of cognitive performance derived from neuropsycholog-
ical research. However, any screening tests for elderly drivers, whether
of eyesight or cognitive abilities, are unlikely to be cost-effective for
two reasons. Firstly, a large number of elderly drivers would need to
be tested in order to identify a minority who posed any risk. Secondly,
because these tests are fairly weak predictors of actual driving performance, you would get unacceptably large numbers of false negative
and false positive results – perfectly safe drivers would be misidenti-
fied as being at risk and vice versa.

Many elderly drivers are aware of their declining abilities. They try
to compensate by restricting themselves to driving conditions that
they feel they can cope with, driving more slowly and leaving larger
safety margins. In many situations, this actually makes them safer
drivers than their younger counterparts.

A study by Read, Kinnear and Weaver (2012) demonstrates this
well. They gave different age groups of participants a whole battery
of visual and cognitive tests, plus a drive in a simulator. On the test
battery, the elderly drivers showed the usual well-documented defi-
cits, such as a narrower UFOV, reduced contrast acuity and slower
reaction times. However, in the simulator, their slower, more cautious
driving style meant that they coped with sudden hazards (such as a
pedestrian stepping out from behind a parked lorry) as well as, if not
better than, younger drivers. In line with many studies, Read et al.'s
work suggests that, while there are age-related declines in visual and
cognitive performance, these are largely negated by the older driver's
greater caution, so that overall, many elderly drivers remain safe.

A notable aspect of Read et al.'s study was the variability in performance amongst the elderly drivers: some of the oldest drivers
had response times within the range of the younger drivers' times.
This variability has often been pointed out by researchers. Hakamies-
Blomqvist suggested that normal healthy ageing is not associated with
any significant decline in driving performance. It's just that with
increasing age, there is a greater risk of experiencing health problems
(such as visual pathology and dementia) that are linked to driving
impairment.

Effectively, as drivers age, there is a growing subset of impaired drivers who are at greater risk of having an accident. Lumping them together with the healthy elderly drivers distorts the apparent level of riskiness for the entire age group. The real problem is to identify the unhealthy drivers and persuade them to give up driving: dangerously impaired older drivers may persist with driving because, just like younger drivers, they have an over-inflated opinion of their driving skills. Some elderly drivers, over the age of 80 or so, do seem to experience particular problems with emerging from junctions. Changes to road design (such as using traffic lights and roundabouts in preference to T-junctions and making road signs larger and more conspicuous) could help to reduce these kinds of accidents. Some studies have also found that driving performance can be improved by training elderly drivers to use compensatory strategies, such as better search patterns at junctions.

Finally, in making comparisons between younger and older drivers, we need to keep in mind that studies often use a cross-sectional design, comparing existing groups of young and old drivers. (The alternative, a longitudinal design in which a single group of drivers is followed during their entire driving lifespan, would be rather tedious to conduct!) These kinds of studies are prone to "cohort effects": elderly drivers differ from younger drivers in many ways other than just chronological age. When today's elderly drivers learnt to drive, the driving test was easier, the roads were less congested and there were fewer high-speed roads.

Cohort effects may account for why very elderly women drivers seem to be a particularly accident-prone group. Many of today's elderly women may have passed their test long ago but left the driving to their husbands. It is known that highly practiced skills deteriorate more slowly than ones which are little-practiced. If these elderly women drive now, they may well be old but very inexperienced drivers, who have had little practice at driving. When elderly drivers have an accident, it is tempting to blame it on their age, but they might never have been competent drivers in the first place!

5

PERSONALITY AND DRIVING

INTRODUCTION

Even within a group of drivers of a particular age and gender, some
are more prone to having accidents than others. It seems likely that
personality characteristics play an important role in this. However,
in practice, it is surprisingly difficult to find any clear relationships
between personality measures and driving performance. While many
studies have found *some* link between one or more personality factors
and accident rates, the relationships are usually not very strong. One
reason is that there is usually so much imprecision or "noise" in the
data that any underlying relationship is hard to detect.

PROBLEMS IN MEASURING PERSONALITY

One source of noise comes from the difficulties involved in measuring personality. We all have our intuitions about personality, but that's
not a sound basis for scientific investigation. For psychologists, personality traits are essentially statistical constructs, derived from differences in how people respond to questionnaire items. For example,
the Eysenck Personality Questionnaire contains items such as "Do

you like going out a lot?" and "Do you prefer reading to meeting people?" Introverts will respond "no" and "yes" respectively, whereas extraverts will respond in the opposite way.

Personality traits defined in this way do not necessarily correspond to our subjective impressions of what constitutes "personality", nor do they necessarily correspond exactly to the underlying dimensions on which individuals really differ. For example, the personality dimensions of extraversion, sensation seeking and impulsivity all seem to be differentiable to some extent, but they also seem to overlap. As a result, a questionnaire that is intended to measure "extraversion" may measure this dimension to some extent, but the overall score might well be contaminated with responses prompted by the other factors. The net result is an imperfect measure of extraversion.

Even if a personality test does measure a unitary trait, it is possible that some aspects of that trait might be conducive to safe driving but not others. Lajunen (2001) points out that some aspects of "neuroticism" (such as anxiety while driving and moodiness) might be associated with *poorer* driving because they increase the number of errors a driver makes, whereas others (for example, being a worrier) might make a person a *safer* driver by increasing his or her concern for safety.

Finally, individuals' behaviour is not determined solely by their stable personality *traits*; it's also affected by the *situation* in which they find themselves. Someone who is high on aggressiveness as a personality trait may not be aggressive all the time but may be more prone to aggression in certain situations (such as being stuck in traffic). This, again, will add imprecision to the data.

PROBLEMS IN MEASURING ACCIDENT RATES

Another source of noise in the data comes from problems in assessing riskiness. On an individual level, accidents are rare. In the UK, roughly 186,000 serious accidents every year are spread over 37 million licensed drivers. Because officially recorded accidents occur at such low frequencies, researchers end up with very little data to work with, even if they have a very large sample of drivers (and most do not). Many researchers try to circumvent this problem by using self-report measures. They may ask drivers about their history of accidents and near-misses during a certain time period, say the past three years. Alternatively, they may ask drivers how often they perform risky behaviours (such as speeding or running red lights) or ask them about their attitudes towards such behaviours.

There is evidence that self-reported risky behaviours are related to accident rates. De Winter and Dodou (2010) combined the data from 70 studies that used James Reason's "Driver Behaviour Questionnaire". This asks for details of errors (mistakes while driving), lapses (forgetting to do something, such as cancelling the indicators after making a turn) and violations (instances of deliberately flouting the law, such as running a red light). Many researchers have claimed that there is an important distinction between errors and lapses (collectively) and violations, with the latter being more predictive of self-reported accident rates. De Winter and Dodou found that overall, the greater the number of violations or errors, the higher the number of self-reported accidents, although the relationship wasn't very strong in absolute terms. These overall effects were influenced by age and gender, in line with the well-established findings that the number of violations (but not errors) decreases with age and that males typically commit more violations and fewer errors than females. Violations were a stronger predictor of accidents for young drivers than for older ones.

The problem with self-report measures is that they can be unreliable, either because the drivers have poor memories or because they want to present themselves in a good light. In Chapter 3, I described Chapman and Underwood's (2000) study, which showed that drivers forgot 80% of near-accidents within a fortnight of their occurrence. Greaves and Ellison (2011) gave 133 Sydney drivers a personality test and asked them about their speeding behaviour. These drivers then had a GPS device inserted in their vehicle for five weeks, purportedly as part of a study on "traffic planning". The correlation between self-reported and actual speeding behaviour was rather poor, with a number of drivers considerably under- or over-estimating how much time they spent speeding.

Single outcome measures may hide important differences between groups of participants. Musselwhite (2006) gave 1,655 UK drivers a questionnaire about what is ostensibly a single "risky" behaviour: speeding. By including questions about the context within which speeding occurred, Musselwhite was able to show that his participants fell into four groups. The largest group took risks unintentionally. The other three groups consisted of a "reactive" group, who took risks when reacting to stress or when they were in a hurry; a "calculated risk" group, who took risks when they thought it was safe to do so (such as late at night or when they were late); and a "continuous risk" group, who frequently took risks for their own sake. The continuous risk group were the youngest (mean age 26 years) and consisted mainly of males. The unintentional risk group were the oldest (mean age 42 years).

Finally, because even high-risk drivers have relatively few accidents, most studies fail to break down participants' accident rates by type of accident. However, different kinds of accident might be associated with different personality types. If so, there might well be a genuine relationship between a certain aspect of personality and a specific kind of accident, but this relationship could be masked by the inclusion of the other kinds of accidents to which that particular personality attribute is not related.

PERSONALITY THEORIES

Most personality theorists attempt to interpret normal behavioural variability in terms of a limited number of dimensions or "traits". An individual's personality results from the amount of each trait that he or she possesses. Estimates of the number of traits varies, but the current consensus is that five factors are sufficient to explain most aspects of personality, as exemplified in Paul Costa and Robert McCrae's extremely popular OCEAN model. These five factors are usually described as openness, conscientiousness, extraversion, agreeableness and neuroticism. (Each of these traits breaks down into separate "facets", which can in turn be measured.)

While other models of personality exist, most driving research has either used the Big Five model or focused on specific traits, such as sensation seeking, locus of control, impulsivity and aggression. Let's look at all of these in turn, starting with the Big Five dimensions. What are the principal characteristics of each personality trait, and how does each trait relate to driving behaviour in practice?

Extraversion

High extraverts are sociable, adventurous, risk-taking, optimistic and outward-directed. Low extraverts (introverts) are reclusive, aloof, cautious and inward-directed. Extraversion seems to be linked with impulsivity and sensation seeking.

Hans Eysenck's original conception of extraversion was that extraverts are chronically "under-aroused" and so need more external stimulation than introverts. If so, extraverts may seek out stimulation to increase their level of arousal to an optimal one, leading them to be high sensation seekers. They may be less engaged in tasks, especially monotonous ones, and they may be more prone to fatigue (which in itself is a major factor in accidents: see Chapter 6). Conversely, their outward focus might make them pay more attention to their environment and hence show greater awareness of impending hazards.

In practice, numerous studies have associated high levels of extraversion with increased levels of accident involvement, violations and various other measures of risky driving. Clarke and Robertson (2005) looked at the data from 47 studies, trying to relate accident rates to personality factors. Overall, correlations between personality variables and accident rates were very low, but there did appear to be some relationship between extraversion and road accidents. In fact, after gender and age, extraversion seems to be one of the best predictors of driving performance.

Neuroticism

Individuals high on neuroticism are distractible, insecure, tense, impatient, irritated, anxious, pessimistic, self-pitying and resentful. They are inclined to experience negative emotions and have difficulty in dealing with problems. Highly neurotic individuals are inefficient in their attempts to overcome stress and are prone to irrational thinking. Individuals low on neuroticism are calm, secure, relaxed and self-satisfied.

A number of studies have suggested that high neuroticism is associated with risky driving and aggressive driving. The main way in which this personality factor affects driving seems to be indirectly: drivers high in neuroticism may be more distractible (because they are preoccupied with their own anxieties), more stressed, more likely to be in a negative mood and more likely to get angry when provoked. None of these characteristics bodes well for safe driving.

Agreeableness

The personality trait of agreeableness reflects an individual's relationships with other people. Individuals high in agreeableness are trusting, unselfish, empathic, helpful, good-natured and polite. Individuals low in agreeableness are egocentric, antagonistic, tough-minded, manipulative, rude, irritable, aggressive, hostile, competitive, ruthless, confrontational and distrustful.

Although low scores on agreeableness can be related to aggressive behaviour and to driving-related aggression in particular, there are actually few studies that have confirmed this relationship empirically. Clarke and Robertson (2005) suggest that individuals with low agreeableness may be more at risk of an accident because they are more likely to come into conflict with other road-users.

Openness

Individuals high in openness are independent, curious, unconventional, idealistic and imaginative. They are receptive to new experiences and ideas and tolerant of novelty and the unknown. Individuals low in openness are conforming, practical, have narrow interests and are unreceptive to new ideas.

Individuals high in openness are receptive to training. However, they are more open to violating rules and engaging in experimentation and improvisation in routine working environments, all factors which might militate against them being safe drivers.

Benfield, Szlemko and Bell (2007) concluded that the majority of aggressive behaviours exhibited while driving were associated with a low score on the openness scale and low scores on the scales measuring agreeableness and conscientiousness.

Conscientiousness

Individuals high in conscientiousness are responsible, well-organised, dependable, careful, thorough, self-disciplined and goal-directed. Individuals low in conscientiousness are antisocial, disorganised, impulsive, rebellious and careless. Their lack of thoroughness in decision-making is associated with a lack of forward planning. They tend to focus on immediate needs and don't adhere to rules and regulations. A number of researchers have found that high conscientiousness is associated with low accident involvement.

Sensation seeking

Sensation seeking is "a trait defined by the seeking of varied, novel, complex and intense sensations and experiences and the willingness to take physical, social, legal and financial risks for the sake of such experiences" (Zuckerman 1994). Zuckerman suggested that it has four underlying dimensions: "thrill and adventure seeking" (seeking unusual sensations by means of exciting and risky sporting activities); "experience seeking" (seeking novel or unconventional experiences, for example, by means of drug use); "boredom susceptibility" (an aversion to boring or repetitive tasks); and "disinhibition" (a desire for loss of self-control, for example by means of alcohol, party-going, and so on).

There is some controversy over how sensation seeking fits into personality models. The most popular view is that it's not a personality trait in itself but the outcome of a particular profile of scores on the various dimensions of the Big Five model. Compared to low sensation seekers, high sensation seekers seem to be higher on extraversion and openness to experience and lower on conscientiousness and agreeableness.

Sensation seeking shows intriguing parallels with age- and gender-related differences in riskiness: it's higher in males than females; it increases with age up to about 16 years of age and then declines during the early twenties. Jonah (1997) looked at 40 studies that attempted to relate sensation seeking to risky driving behaviours. All but four showed a significant positive relationship between sensation seeking and some aspect of risky driving. While the sensation seeking subscales have not been examined very often, the "thrill and adventure seeking" factor seems to be most strongly related to risky driving behaviour, followed by the "disinhibition" and "experience seeking" components.

Before we get too excited about sensation seeking as a complete explanation for risky driving, however, we should note that correlations between driving behaviour and sensation seeking are typically fairly weak. This means that sensation seeking accounts for only a fraction of the variation in riskiness between drivers. Also, as Arnett (1996) pointed out, reckless behaviours are widespread amongst young drivers, not just high sensation seekers. In Arnett's study of American high school and college students, high sensation seekers were more likely to drive over 80 miles per hour, race other cars and drive while intoxicated. However, over 80% of the students reported engaging in these activities; they may have been committed more often by high sensation seekers, but they were certainly not confined to that group. Clearly "sensation seeking" is only part of the explanation for reckless behaviour in young people.

Locus of control

Locus of control refers to the extent to which people believe that they are in control of their own destiny, as opposed to their fate being determined by external forces. Those with an internal LOC perceive outcomes to depend on their own skills, efforts or behaviour. People with an external LOC believe that they have little control over what happens to them, that it is largely a matter of luck or "fate".

It's hard to make clear predictions about the effects of LOC on accident rates. You could argue that drivers with an internal LOC might drive more riskily, because they have greater belief that they are in control of the situation and hence can avoid accidents by their own actions. However, you could equally argue that drivers with an external LOC might drive more riskily: if they perceive accidents to be largely a matter of luck, then they might take fewer precautions to avoid them.

The empirical data on the effects of LOC are equivocal. Holland, Geraghty and Shah (2010) concluded that this is because studies often fail to take account of other factors that interact with LOC, such as gender and driving experience. Women typically are relatively external in LOC, while men typically show an internal LOC. In common with some previous studies, Holland et al. failed to find any association between LOC and risky driving. However, they make an interesting speculation about how the effects of gender, driving experience and LOC might interact. Young men persist in being riskier drivers than young women, despite having greater experience of driving. Perhaps men's typically internal LOC leads them to believe that they have more control of the situation. Experience may have more effect on women's behaviour because of their relatively external LOC.

Impulsivity

Impulsivity relates to the degree of control people have over their actions. It seems to be related to sensation seeking. Dahlen, Martin, Ragan and Kuhlman (2005) reviewed studies suggesting that high impulsivity is associated with high-risk behaviours, such as drink-driving, moving violations and reduced seatbelt use, and with higher accident rates. Impulsivity has also been linked to anger and aggressiveness.

Anger and aggressiveness

In recent years, there has been considerable media interest in driver aggression, in the form of "road rage". As Dula and Ballard (2003) pointed out, three different aspects of driver behaviour have been labelled as "aggressive" by researchers: intentional acts of physical, verbal or gestured aggression (such as hitting another driver, swearing at others or making an obscene gesture); negative emotions while driving (e.g., anger); and risk taking (such as driving through a red light or changing lanes rapidly). Scores on Jerry Deffenbacher's "Driving Anger Scale" are correlated positively (though weakly) with risky behaviours, such as poor concentration, loss of vehicle control and near-misses while driving. Men score higher than women on these kinds of measures, suggesting that everyday gender differences in aggression extend to driving.

It is arguable whether risk taking should be considered as "aggression" or as a side-effect of it. Aggressiveness and riskiness are certainly correlated to some extent. In Arnett's (1996) study mentioned earlier, aggressiveness was also measured. Various "reckless" behaviours, such as racing and speeding, were moderately correlated with aggressiveness, and in fact, these correlations were not too dissimilar from the correlations between these behaviours and sensation seeking.

One question is whether aggressiveness is a stable personality trait or whether it is triggered by the situation in which the drivers find themselves. The answer is both. Research suggests that there are lifelong, reasonably stable individual differences in aggressiveness, although aggression in men does decline with age and driving experience. However, scores on the Driving Anger Scale correlate only moderately with measures of anger outside of the context of driving, suggesting that an angry driver is not necessarily an angry person in all aspects of his or her life.

Deffenbacher suggests that drivers' aggressiveness arises out of an interaction between "trait" and "state" – i.e., between drivers' propensity for anger and the situation in which they find themselves. In a study investigating driving anger in undergraduate student drivers, there was no correlation at all between drivers' Driving Anger Scale score and their level of anger when they imagined themselves "driving unimpeded on a country road on a beautiful day". However as traffic conditions worsened, so their anger increased. A similar interaction between trait and state anger was found in a study by Deffenbacher and his colleagues of drivers who were receiving counselling for their driving anger. High- and low-anger drivers were similar under low levels of provocation, but as the level of provocation increased, high-anger drivers became much angrier and also reported more aggressive and risky behaviour (Deffenbacher, Huff, Lynch, Oetting and Salvatore 2000).

Lajunen and Parker (2001) cast doubt on the idea that drivers' personalities somehow change when they get in a car; this is unlikely, given what we know about the stability of aggressiveness as a personality trait. Their data suggest that the relationship between anger, verbal and physical aggression and driving is complex and that different situations give rise to different patterns of angry or aggressive responses.

MULTIDIMENSIONAL PERSONALITY PROFILES

For all of these one-dimensional measures of personality characteristics, correlations between test scores and accident rates are usually fairly small. This means knowledge of a person's test score on a single personality measure would, in practice, tell us little about how risky his or her driving is likely to be. Some researchers have therefore attempted to see if personality profiles provide a better guide to driver riskiness.

The Norwegian psychologist Pål Ulleberg was one of the first to investigate if riskiness was related to a constellation of personality measures rather than just one (Ulleberg 2002). He performed a statistical technique called cluster analysis on a battery of measures of personality, attitudes to risk and accident records. This revealed the existence of six clusters of drivers, two of whom were "low risk" and two of whom were "high risk". The members of one of the high-risk groups were characterised by being high on sensation seeking, norm-lessness ("the belief that socially unapproved behaviours are required to achieve certain goals") and driving anger and low on altruism and anxiety. Members of this high-risk group – mostly male – had high scores on risk-taking behaviour, poor attitudes to risk and low risk perception scores. They rated their own driving skills highly but had the highest accident rates of the six clusters. The other high-risk group – mostly female – were high on sensation seeking, aggression, anxiety and anger and low on altruism. They had risky driving habits, poor attitudes to road safety and high accident rates. Members of this cluster did not rate their own driving skills as very good, and they perceived their risk of an accident as high.

Fabio Lucidi and his colleagues at the University of Rome performed a similar analysis to Ulleberg's, except they also included a measure of locus of control. Lucidi et al. identified three clusters: "risky", "worried" and "careful" drivers. The "risky" cluster were mainly male and characterised by high levels of external LOC, norm-lessness, excitement-seeking and driving-related anger, plus low levels of anxiety and altruism. This cluster resembled one of Ulleberg's two high-risk clusters. Compared to the other two groups, the "risky" group had more driving convictions, more accidents, more negative attitudes to road safety, higher scores on the "violations" subscale of the DBQ and a stronger belief that they were at less risk of being involved in an accident.

The other two clusters were similar to Ulleberg et al.'s low-risk clusters. The "worried" cluster contained more females than males. They were high in anxiety and driving anger but lower on normless-ness, excitement-seeking and external LOC than the "risky" drivers. They had fewer violations and convictions than the "risky" group but as many lapses. These drivers were the ones who felt most at risk of being involved in a traffic accident. Lucidi et al. suggest that these drivers' high levels of anxiety and their heightened perception of being at risk of an accident, combined with their perception that they have little control over traffic situations, might all conspire to decrease their risk-taking attitudes and risky driving compared to the "risky" group. The "careful" driver cluster consisted of roughly equal numbers of males and females. Members of this group scored high on emotional stability and had low levels of driving anger and excitement-seeking. They were midway between the other two groups in terms of anxiety, and they had the highest altruism scores and lowest normlessness scores. They also had a high internal LOC. Their attitudes to road safety were more positive, and they had lower levels of violations, errors and lapses and had had fewer accidents.

In Germany, Philipp Herzberg performed a cluster analysis of personality scores and identified three "types" of driver. "Resilient" drivers were low on neuroticism and above average on the other four scales. "Overcontrolled" drivers were high on neuroticism and conscientiousness, average on agreeableness and low on extraversion and openness. "Undercontrolled" drivers were high on neuroticism and openness, low on conscientiousness and agreeableness and average on extraversion.

The three types differed on a number of measures; 56% of the drivers in the overcontrolled group and 43% of those in the resilient group had never had an accident, whereas this was true for only 23% of the undercontrolled group. The undercontrolled group also had the highest number of drivers with more than one accident. In terms of past convictions, 81% of the overcontrolled drivers had clean licences, compared to 60% in both the resilient and undercontrolled groups. Twice as many undercontrollers had received four or more fines compared to the other groups, and 30% of the undercontrollers had been banned from driving compared to only 19% of the overcontrolled group. The undercontrolled drivers were the most likely to drink and drive, and the resilient drivers were the least likely to do so.

CONCLUSIONS

Research clearly indicates that personality variables influence self-reported driver *behaviour*. The evidence that personality affects *accident rates* is less strong. One reason for this is that the data are so messy, which makes finding relationships extremely difficult. Drivers' behaviour is not determined solely by their personality traits but by the *interaction* between those traits and the situations in which they find themselves. Also, whether risky driving ends in disaster is not determined solely by how a driver behaves. Other drivers may compensate for someone's bad driving, and luck plays a part too. In any event, driver behaviour seems to be better predicted by a personality *profile* (i.e., individual differences across a spectrum of personality attributes) rather than by any single personality measure.

A further complication is that different personality characteristics may be associated with different *types* of risky driving behaviour. One reason why personality measures are not strong predictors of driver behaviour might be because measures of "risky driving" have been too broad. For example, Fernandes, Job and Hatfield (2007) found that whereas speeding was predicted by high scores on a measure of "authority-rebellion", drink-driving was predicted by high scores on quite different measures, such as sensation seeking and "optimism bias" (the belief that compared to others, you are more likely to experience pleasant things and less likely to experience unpleasant ones). Future research in this area might profit from considering how personality affects specific driving behaviours, rather than behaviour in general.

6

DRIVING WHILE IMPAIRED

INTRODUCTION

People drive when they are tired, after drinking alcohol or taking drugs (not just illicit ones) or when they feel ill (maybe because of the alcohol they drank the night before). Obviously, all of these things will affect driving performance if taken to the extreme, and in fact, fatigue and drink-driving are major contributors to the accident statistics. But how risky is the slightly tired driver or the one who has drunk alcohol but only up to the legal limit?

FATIGUE

The prevalence of fatigue-related accidents

It's hard to know how many accidents are caused by fatigue. As well as directly causing accidents, fatigue is likely to be involved in many crashes that are attributed to some more obvious factor. Reviews of accident statistics suggest that fatigue contributes to about a quarter of all fatal crashes. This is mainly because drivers are most likely to fall asleep on monotonous, high-speed roads. Interestingly, younger drivers tend to fall asleep in the early hours of the morning, whereas older drivers tend to fall asleep in the afternoon. There are also individual differences in susceptibility to fatigue, with extraverts and high sensa-tion seekers being more susceptible than introverts and low sensation seekers, respectively.

Obstructive sleep apnoea is a major risk factor for fatigue-related accidents. In this condition, the sleeper's throat relaxes, restricting breathing. Because the interruptions to sleep are brief, sufferers may not know that they are sleeping poorly, but they will be aware of feeling sleepy during the day. A review by Chamara Senaratna and his colleagues (2017) concluded that mild OSA is widespread, affecting as many as 38% of the general population. At clinical levels (where driving is likely to be significantly impaired by daytime drowsiness), OSA could affect up to 17% of the population. OSA is a growing problem in developed countries, as it's linked to obesity. It's also more common in males and the elderly. Senaratna et al. estimate that about 90% of male drivers aged over 60 have mild OSA and about half have it at clinical levels.

Fatigue-related accidents are a particular problem for professional drivers. Although subject to regulations about how long they can drive (in the European Union at least), long-distance lorry drivers work long shifts, often interspersed with little or poor sleep, and they drive for prolonged periods on monotonous high-speed roads, often at night. There are no restrictions at all on the maximum work-ing hours for many professional drivers, such as taxi drivers, sales representatives – and driving instructors!

Compared to the accident statistics, studies of drivers' self-reports tend to give higher estimates of the frequency with which drivers feel dangerously tired, presumably because they include episodes of fatigue that have led to a near-miss or minor accident, not just more serious accidents. These studies suggest that most drivers have expe-rienced troublesome fatigue at some point while driving. Between a quarter and a half of drivers say that they have at some time fallen asleep while driving, and up to 10% of drivers admit that they have had an accident as a result of falling asleep.

As with the accident statistics, questionnaire studies suggest that the problem of fatigue is more serious for professional drivers. In a UK survey by Maycock (1997), nearly 60% of company car drivers said they had felt close to falling asleep whilst driving. A study of American long-distance lorry drivers by Anne McCartt and her colleagues found that 47% had fallen asleep at the wheel at some point. Sagberg et al. (2004) concluded that fatigue-related accidents accounted for up to 41% of all truck-drivers' accidents and up to 30% of their fatal ones.

Psychological theories of sleep and fatigue

So far, I've talked about "fatigue", but what exactly is it? "Sleepiness" and "fatigue" are often used interchangeably, but they don't neces-sarily refer to the same thing. "Sleepiness" is of course produced by a lack of sleep. Most individuals need at least four to five hours of sleep a night, although there are large individual differences. Habit plays a part, and some degree of sleep deprivation can be tolerated fairly well, at least in the short term. Sleep goes through a number of stages: it begins with stages 1 and 2, which are light sleep, and then progresses to stages 3 and 4 of deep sleep. Unlike the preceding stages, stage 5 sleep involves rapid eye movements, which is why it is usually called REM sleep. It's also known as "paradoxical" sleep, because in terms of brain activity, it is more like being awake than the non-REM stages. Most dreaming seems to occur during this stage. The whole cycle of sleep stages is repeated about five times each night.

Loss of stage 3 and 4 sleep is associated with feeling physically tired and is the type of sleep which sleep-deprived individuals most desire. The fact that loss of REM sleep produces compensatory "rebound" effects (so you have more REM sleep the next time you sleep) would suggest it is important; however, in practice, loss of REM sleep appears to do little other than make people more irritable.

Although the amount and quality of sleep are important determi-nants of sleepiness, so too is an individual's circadian rhythm. Most people have two "troughs" per day, times when they feel sleepiest. One is early in the morning (3–4 a.m.), and the other is mid-afternoon after lunch. These two troughs can be seen in driving simulator studies and are also reflected in the road accident statistics.

"Fatigue" is much harder to define. Unlike sleep, "fatigue" does not seem to be clearly associated with any detectable physiological changes. It's generally defined in terms of its consequences: a reluctance to continue an activity that has been performed for some time, a loss of concentration and subjective tiredness and discomfort. By making a "mental effort", it's possible to overcome fatigue-related performance decline, at least for a short time. However, with increasing fatigue comes increasing reluctance to apply the extra effort. It is not clear what this "effort" actually involves. As the cognitive scientist Harold Pashler pointed out, the increased activity in the brain's frontal regions that is produced by thinking is quite small compared with the large amount of activity produced in posterior brain regions by passive viewing. Hence watching TV should consume more energy (and be more fatiguing) than problem-solving!

How fatigue affects driving performance

Drivers' performance is likely to be affected by *when* they drive (i.e., at what point they are active within their circadian cycle); *how long* they have been driving (their "time on task"); and how tired they were before they began (which depends on how much sleep or rest they obtained previously). As Thiffault and Bergeron (2003) pointed out, these are all "endogenous" factors, related to the driver's internal state. Driving performance is also affected by "exogenous" influences, such as the degree of environmental stimulation. Thiffault and Bergeron demonstrated this experimentally. Participants performed two 40-minute sessions of simulator "driving" during the "post-lunch dip" in their circadian cycle. In both sessions, the road was a predominantly straight two-lane highway. However, in one session, the road was flanked by endless pine trees and thus was very predictable and monotonous. In the other session, the surroundings were more varied: the road went over bridges and overpasses, and the driver sporadically encountered people, trees, houses and road signs. In both sessions, performance steadily deteriorated over time but more so when the environment was monotonous.

For accidents in which drivers have been so tired that they have fallen asleep and lost control of the vehicle, it seems fairly obvious how fatigue has affected behaviour. However, what are the effects of less dramatic levels of fatigue? Modern theories propose that individuals have a limited pool of resources which can be allocated to different tasks in a flexible and dynamic way. For example, Glyn Hockey's "compensatory control" theory suggests individuals monitor their behaviour and attempt to maintain performance at acceptable levels. If necessary, this is achieved by preserving performance on "primary" tasks at the expense of "secondary" ones. Thus a fatigued driver might focus on the primary aspects of driving (lane-keeping and obstacle avoidance) by dispensing with allocating resources to secondary aspects (such as using the mirrors and indicators).

This is supported by empirical studies of how fatigue affects drivers. Initially, there is increasingly selective attention: fatigued drivers focus on their internal state rather than the surroundings and tend to concentrate on the most important tasks (such as lane maintenance and keeping a safe distance from the vehicle in front) at the expense of less important ones. Visual sampling of the environment becomes dominated by expectations, and the field of view tends to become increasingly narrow. Counter-intuitively, fatigued individuals often show preserved performance on complex tasks but not simple ones, so driving is most likely to be affected when it appears to be most straightforward.

As fatigue progresses, drivers start to experience "microsleeps" of about half to one and a half seconds. On a motorway, microsleeps are long enough to alarm a driver because the vehicle will drift in its lane, but they are short enough for the driver to stand a chance of regaining control. On the approach to a bend or on a two-lane road with traffic approaching from the opposite direction, microsleeps may have more unfortunate consequences.

By this point, drivers are well aware that they are falling asleep, but they often try to press on regardless. They try to stave off sleep by using various strategies to increase self-stimulation (such as singing, hitting themselves or opening the window to get more fresh air). Horne and Reyner (1996) found the most effective short-term counter-measure was for drivers to take a 10 to 15 minute nap plus 150 to 200 milligrams of caffeine. However, by this stage, the onset of sleep is inevitable, and the only truly safe course of action is to stop driving.

An interesting but relatively under-researched phenomenon is "highway hypnosis" or "driving without attention mode". The driver drives automatically, as if on "autopilot". It seems to be an intermediate state between wakefulness and sleepiness, one that precedes microsleeps. It is almost like sleeping with one's eyes open – and as such, highly dangerous.

DRUGS

Complications in assessing the effects of drugs on driving

It's very difficult to get a clear idea of how any particular drug might affect driving performance. Acute effects of a single dose on undergraduate volunteers may differ from the long-term effects of prolonged use. Habitual use may produce tolerance (so that a single dose has less effect), but it can also lead to long-term damage. Permanent cognitive impairment has been demonstrated for users of "crack" cocaine, methadone, MDMA ("Ecstasy") and alcohol. For ethical reasons, many studies compare a group of drug users to a group of non-users. The problem with this is that any observed differences in driving performance may be due at least in part to "cohort effects": drug users and non-users may differ in many respects other than the presence of the drug, such as personality, attitudes towards risk-taking, sensation seeking, general health and so on.

A well-designed, carefully controlled laboratory study may be able to detect subtle effects of a drug on performance even at very low doses. However, we want to know whether these effects really have any practical relevance to real-world driving. Epidemiological studies can help here, but it is difficult to establish a reliable baseline against which to measure drug effects. To assess the riskiness of drug use while driving, it's not enough to know how often it occurs in drivers who have crashed; we need to know how many drivers are taking the drug and not crashing. One solution is to use a case-control method. A sample of drivers involved in a crash is compared to a similar sample who have not crashed. If drugs are found to be more common in the former group, it implies that the drugs played a role in their accidents. In a variant of this technique, "culpability analysis", dead or injured drivers are categorised according to whether they were responsible for their crash. The prevalence of drug use in each group is then assessed.

Drugs may impair driving performance directly, by affecting cognitive and motor performance, or indirectly by influencing mood. For example, cocaine may lead to increased aggressiveness, especially in combination with alcohol. Amphetamines and MDMA are associated with greater impulsivity. Addicts who are in a state of withdrawal are unlikely to be concentrating on their driving.

In real life, people often use more than one drug at the same time. For example, MDMA, cannabis and cocaine are frequently used together with alcohol. There's good evidence that cannabis has additive effects when combined with alcohol, leading to a greatly increased risk of a crash compared to when cannabis is used on its own.

Except in the case of alcohol and cannabis, it is difficult to know for certain whether someone has taken a drug, let alone how recently he or she took it. This makes it hard to assess the accident risk associated with a particular drug. On the one hand, there might be underestimation of the prevalence of drug-taking amongst drivers. Many drugs are difficult to detect in urine. Blood tests are more effective, but they will not be taken except in the case of serious or fatal accidents. Stimulants, such as cocaine and MDMA, may be undetectable 12 hours after use. Underestimation of the prevalence of drug-taking amongst drivers could lead to an *overestimation* of the apparent risks of drugged-driving (because there are actually more drugged drivers on the roads *not* having accidents than we thought).

In the case of cannabis, earlier investigations sometimes failed to differentiate between its active ingredient, Δ^9 – tetrahydrocannabinol (THC), and its inactive metabolites. The inactive metabolites may be detectable in drug tests long after the drug's psychotropic effects have worn off. Therefore, a study could end up with a "cannabis-using" sample that included many drivers who were not actually impaired by THC at the time they were driving – thus leading to underestimation of the accident risk posed by cannabis.

Finally, illicit drug use and accidents are both fairly rare. Most studies therefore end up with just a handful of drug-using drivers who have had an accident. It is difficult to find reliable evidence of increased accident risk when sample sizes are this small.

The effects of drugs on driving performance

For reasons of space, I'll confine discussion here to the three most commonly used drugs that are likely to affect driving: alcohol, cannabis and tranquilisers.

Alcohol

Statistical analyses show clearly that alcohol consumption is associated with a greatly elevated risk of having an accident and experimental findings give some insight into why this is so. Ethanol, the type of alcohol present in alcoholic drinks, produces a generalised depression of the central nervous system. This leads initially to euphoria, because alcohol depresses inhibitory synapses in the brain before it affects excitatory ones. (Depression of inhibition is effectively equivalent to excitation). As alcohol levels increase, both sorts of synapse are depressed, and the state of euphoria is progressively lost. At higher doses, the ability to think clearly is affected, judgement is impaired and mood becomes unstable.

Alcohol begins to affect the central nervous system within minutes of being drunk. If no further alcohol is taken, peak blood alcohol levels are reached within an hour and then the total alcohol content of the body starts to decrease linearly. For many drugs, the rate of metabolism by the liver depends on the drug's concentration in the bloodstream: the higher the concentration, the faster it's metabolised. However, alcohol is metabolised at a slow, constant rate, largely independently of its concentration in the bloodstream and hence, independently of the amount consumed. BAC can be expressed in various ways. In the UK, it is usually in terms of the weight of alcohol in 100 millilitres of blood (mg/100ml); thus the UK legal limit for drinking and driving is 80 mg/100 ml blood. In terms of the percentage (by weight) of alcohol in the blood, 80 mg/100 ml corresponds to a BAC of 0.08%, 100 mg/100 ml corresponds to 0.10% and so on.

Alcohol affects all aspects of driving performance but to different extents depending on the dose. It impairs judgement, so that drunk drivers may overestimate their abilities. Manoeuvres may be attempted (such as overtaking and fast cornering) that would be rejected by a sober driver as being too risky. Drunk drivers also tend to drive faster than they would when sober.

The perceptual level is also affected. In large doses, alcohol impairs visual acuity, but attention is affected long before this. Drunk drivers have reduced cognitive capacity to deal with the many task demands of driving; to compensate, they may select certain tasks as primary at the expense of others. They may concentrate on steering and other aspects of vehicle control, firstly because they are the most immediate demands on the driver and secondly because the drunk driver wants to evade detection by the police. The result is reduced attention to the surroundings (and hence to potential accident threats and hazards).

At the motor level, relatively automatised actions, such as steering, are impaired by alcohol but not as much as "higher" processes (at least, not until the person is very drunk). This probably reinforces the drunk drivers' delusion that they are capable of driving.

Numerous reviews of pure and applied research (for example Moskowitz and Fiorentino 2000), all point to similar conclusions. "Automatic" behaviours (over-learnt tasks which require little conscious mental activity, such as simple tracking and measures of reaction time) are relatively unaffected by alcohol until BAC reaches

0.05% or so. However, "controlled" behaviours (tasks which involve a greater mental workload, such as difficult tracking, divided-attention tasks, information-processing and so on) are affected at much lower BAC's, 0.01% or less. The most relevant tests on the effects of alcohol are those involving actual driving and flying, either in real life or in simulators. Reviewing 25 studies of this kind, Moskowitz and Fiorentino reported that nearly all of them found impairment by low levels of alcohol.

Alcohol also produces drowsiness. Moskowitz and Fiorentino report that tests of wakefulness are affected by BACs as low as 0.01%. People who drink and drive are also likely to be fatigued because they are likely to be driving late at night. Jim Horne and his group at the Loughborough Sleep Research Centre conducted a number of studies looking at how the effects of alcohol interact with drivers' circadian rhythms. Alcohol was found to be about twice as potent during the peak times for sleepiness (4:00 to 6:00 a.m. and 2:00 to 4:00 p.m.) than at other times. Even small amounts of alcohol could dangerously impair driving if taken in the afternoon. Horne and his colleagues suggest that the more one suffers from the afternoon "dip" in alertness, the more potent the effects of alcohol will be at that time. In one study, they tested young male drivers' performance in a driving simulator, after they had consumed an amount of alcohol that was equivalent to half that permitted by UK law. Both alcohol and sleep restriction impaired performance to some extent, but when combined, they significantly increased the amount of lane drifting. Interestingly, this additive effect of alcohol and sleepiness was apparent in the participants' EEG recordings but not in their subjective ratings of sleepiness, suggesting they were unaware that alcohol had dangerously increased their level of sleepiness.

Moskowitz and Fiorentino concluded there is strong evidence that impairment of some driving-related skills can be found when there is *any* departure from 0 BAC. By 0.05%, most of the studies that they reviewed had found some alcohol-induced impairment. By BAC's of 0.08%, 94% of the studies had reported impairment. Virtually all participants tested in these studies showed impairment on some critical driving measure once a BAC of 0.08% was reached – and recall that this is the legal limit for drink-driving in the UK and many other countries. However, the general impression is clearly one of progressive impairment as the BAC increases; there is no "threshold" for the effects of alcohol, below which performance is unimpaired and above which it is affected.

Moskowitz and Fiorentio point out that their review does not include studies of driver emotion, motivation and judgement, but these are important aspects of driving too.

What should be the legal limit of alcohol for drivers?

In the UK, the Road Safety Act of 1967 made the legal limit for drinking and driving 80 milligrams per 100 millilitres of blood (0.08%), at which level it has remained (except in Scotland, where in 2014, it was reduced to 0.05%). Most European states have 0.08% or 0.05% limits. In the United States, most states have a legal BAC limit of 0.10% and a minority have a limit of 0.08%. Some states have a lower limit or even zero tolerance for younger or professional drivers.

These so-called "*per se*" laws define intoxication purely in terms of BAC. This makes it much easier to convict drunk drivers, because the prosecution do not have to provide convincing evidence of any behavioural impairment. Unfortunately, a legal drink-drive limit gives the false impression that there is some kind of threshold above which driving is impaired and below which it is not. It makes no allowance for the large individual differences in the rate of alcohol absorption into the bloodstream and variations in the magnitude of its subjective effects. Consequently, some drivers will be dangerously impaired well before they reach a 0.08% BAC. Really, the legal limit is quite arbitrary; the effects of alcohol on performance are dose-dependent, and the accident risk increases steeply with increasing dosage.

On the basis of an extensive review of research, Killoran, Cunning, Doyle and Sheppard (2010) concluded that driving after *any* alcohol increases the risk of an accident. Drivers with a BAC between 0.02% and 0.05% are three times more likely to have a fatal accident than a sober driver. They are six times more likely if they have a BAC between 0.05 to 0.08% and 11 times more likely if their BAC is between 0.08 and 0.10%. Killoran and her colleagues concluded there was strong evidence that reducing the BAC limit to 0.05% had produced significant and long-lasting effects on accident rates in those countries which had already done so and that these changes were particularly effective in reducing accident rates for young drivers. Their cautious estimate was that reducing the BAC limit in England and Wales to 0.05% would save up to 168 deaths and 15,832 injuries every year.

Cannabis

After alcohol, cannabis is the most commonly found drug in the blood of motorists involved in accidents in the US, Australia and most European countries. Unlike most illicit drugs, cannabis is used widely enough and is sufficiently innocuous for there to exist numerous experimental studies of its effects on behaviour. Attempts have also been made to use accident statistics in order to assess its riskiness for drivers. However, as mentioned earlier, this is complicated by the lack of a clear indicator of recent use.

The physiological effects of cannabis

The active ingredient in cannabis is Δ^9 – tetrahydrocannabinol (THC). THC starts to take effect within minutes after smoking begins, and peak blood concentrations occur within 10 to 30 minutes. Unless more is smoked, the effects seldom last longer than about 2 to 3 hours. THC is almost completely metabolised to less active products by the liver before it is excreted; these metabolites are detectable in a heavy smoker for about a month after smoking has stopped. At low to moderate doses, THC is a mild sedative-hypnotic resembling alcohol and the benzodiazepines. Unlike these drugs, however, higher doses of THC may produce euphoria, hallucinations and heightened sensation, similar to a mild LSD experience. A problem for users (and experimenters!) is that the amount of THC ingested depends heavily not just on the potency of the cannabis itself but on how it is smoked (e.g., frequency and depth of inhalation), leading to wide individual differences in the effects of apparently similar doses.

Experimental and epidemiological studies of the effects of cannabis

Experimental studies on the effects of cannabis on driving performance are consistent in showing that THC impairs cognition, psychomotor performance and actual driving performance, in a dose-related manner – the higher the dosage of THC, the worse performance becomes. THC impairs some aspects of driving more than others; highly automated behaviours, such as road tracking, appear to be affected by THC to a greater extent than more complex driving tasks requiring conscious control.

Curiously, although cannabis produces detectable cognitive and motor impairments in the laboratory, there's less evidence that driving after using cannabis is associated with an increased risk of accident involvement. One possible explanation lies in the way in which cannabis affects performance, which is somewhat different from the effects of alcohol. Unlike drink-drivers, cannabis-using drivers may be quite aware that they are impaired and therefore compensate by driving more slowly and cautiously. However, cannabis does slow RT on "secondary" tasks during simulated driving, suggesting that distraction might be important in cannabis-related collisions.

However, as mentioned earlier, given the long persistence of cannabis metabolites, it may be that many studies have failed to detect any effects of cannabis on driving because they have included drivers who tested positive for the presence of cannabis but who were not actively under its influence at the time of their accident. Drummer et al. (2004) reported the results of a 10-year culpability study which attempted to assess the effects of drug use on the likelihood of Australian drivers being responsible for their fatal crashes. Users of alcohol and cannabis (as reflected in THC levels in blood samples) were more likely to have been responsible for their accidents, and there was clear evidence of a dose-response relationship: the more alcohol or cannabis they had consumed, the more likely drivers were to have caused their accident.

Drummer et al. found that THC concentrations of 0.5 nanograms per millilitre (ng/ml) or higher produced odds ratios for accident culpability similar to those for drivers with a BAC of at least 0.15%. Drummer et al. suggest that cannabis does have significant effects on driving performance, but only for the relatively short time that the driver has a blood concentration of 5 ng/ml or more. Ramaekers et al. (2004) drew similar conclusions from their review of epidemiological studies: they noted that results from the few surveys which confirmed recent use of cannabis (by directly measuring THC levels in blood, as opposed to measuring inactive metabolites) demonstrated clearly that accident-involved cannabis users were between three and seven times more likely to be responsible for their crash.

Thus the link between cannabis use and an increased risk of a road accident may well be stronger than it appears from most of the epidemiological literature. It has been suggested that at least some of this elevated accident risk may stem not so much from the pharmacological effects of cannabis but from users' tendency to have a generally reckless driving style. While personality characteristics of cannabis users may certainly play a role, there are reasons to doubt that this is the major reason for their increased accident risk. For one thing, if impulsiveness or recklessness produced a predisposition both to cannabis use and risky driving, then there should be a stronger association between *past* cannabis use and crash involvement than has in fact been found. Personality traits tend to be reasonably stable over time, so someone who was impulsive enough to use cannabis in the past should still be impulsive now (and hence still at risk of a crash). However the available evidence suggests that only *recent* use of cannabis is linked to accidents, so it is more plausible to attribute the increased crash risk to the effects of the drug itself.

Tranquilisers

Tranquilisers are likely to impair driving ability; the psychological effects of barbiturates are generally similar to those produced by alcohol, ranging from euphoria to sleep, depending on the concentration. As with alcohol, a person's mood is important; barbiturates can produce aggression or depression, depending on the person's surroundings. Impaired judgement occurs well before the person is noticeably intoxicated. Many laboratory studies show that benzodiazepines increase reaction times, decrease target detection, impair performance on tasks involving motor control or coordination and disrupt both real and simulated driving. The effects of some of the benzodiazepines are quite long-lasting, so that people who use a benzodiazepine as a sedative may still be affected the following morning when they drive to work.

Vingilis and Macdonald (2002) reviewed the effects of benzodiazepines on driving and concluded that there is both epidemiological and experimental evidence to suggest that benzodiazepine use is associated with an increased risk of having an accident. A benzodiazepine user is up to six times more likely to be in a crash than a non-user, the risk depending on the particular type of benzodiazepine used.

Assessment of the effects of tranquilisers is complicated by the fact that most studies have used acute drug doses in healthy young volunteers: tolerance develops with prolonged use, so these studies may have overestimated the degree of impairment that would be experienced by long-term users. Importantly, the sedative effects of many of the barbiturates and benzodiazepines can be greatly exacerbated by alcohol; a small amount of alcohol plus a small amount of barbiturate may produce a much greater effect than one would expect by calculating the effect of each drug individually.

CONCLUSIONS

Fatigue and alcohol are two of the biggest causes of fatal accidents. Although it's difficult to estimate the prevalence of fatigue-related accidents with any degree of accuracy, it seems reasonably clear that driving while fatigued is a widespread phenomenon and that it can lead to accidents both directly (because drivers fall asleep at the wheel and lose control of the vehicle) and indirectly (by causing drivers to concentrate more on trying to stay awake and less on their surroundings).

It is difficult to make firm statements about how likely fatigue is to occur, because it depends on the interaction of so many different factors, such as a driver's internal state (their circadian rhythm and how much decent sleep they have had recently), the time of day and external factors, such as how monotonous the journey is. There have been attempts to produce warning systems to alert drivers to the fact that they are fatigued. These have been unsuccessful, mainly because objective measures, such as lane-keeping accuracy and blink frequency or duration are only poorly correlated with the driver's internal state. In any case, this line of research seems to be ill-conceived because drivers generally know when they are fatigued – the trouble is that they overestimate the extent to which they can overcome it. The real problem is how to persuade drivers to stop driving once they become fatigued. This is especially difficult in the case of professional drivers, because their job may not permit them to stop and rest.

When it comes to drugs, alcohol is by far the biggest threat to road safety, both because it is widely used and because of its extensive effects on performance: not only does it impair cognitive and motor abilities, but it affects drivers' judgement and increases risk-taking. The latter is particularly unfortunate because alcohol abuse is more common amongst young male drivers, who are more likely to drive riskily anyway. Alcohol is unequivocally a major cause of road accidents. Epidemiological studies are unanimous in demonstrating that the risk of an accident is significantly increased even by moderate levels of alcohol (well below the 0.08% legal limit in England and Wales) and that high blood alcohol levels are associated with a greatly increased risk of crashing.

It is difficult to make accurate assessments of the risks associated with other drugs. Partly this is because their misuse is not nearly as widespread as that of alcohol. There is also the complication that they are often used together with alcohol, so that any impairment is at least in part attributable to the latter. However, it's safe to say that most illicit drugs, including cannabis, produce a detectable impairment in driving performance that is likely to increase the risk of an accident.

Illicit drugs are not the only drugs that affect driving, however; many prescription and over-the-counter medicines can impair performance, especially in conjunction with alcohol. A multidisciplinary panel of experts convened by the US National Highway Traffic Safety Administration to discuss drugged-driving (Kay and Logan, 2011) concluded that many legal drugs have the potential to affect driving but that their effects were poorly understood. The panel highlighted the need to establish a set of systematic procedures for assessing the safety of drugs with respect to driving. These could be based on a drug's known physiological effects, epidemiological data and standardised assessments of aspects of behaviour that are relevant to driving (e.g., tests of alertness, attention and on-road driving performance).

Finally, there is a clear need for drivers to be better educated about how fatigue and drugs can affect driving. Many young drivers are aware of the risks of alcohol but seriously underestimate the risks of cannabis. There is widespread ignorance about how "units" of alcohol correspond to alcoholic drinks. In the UK, the drugged-driving law sets legal "thresholds" for a number of common medications (such as tranquilisers) but there is little guidance on how these thresholds equate to commonly prescribed dosages of the medicines in question.

7

THE FUTURE OF DRIVING

INTRODUCTION

In May 2016, Joshua Brown was killed when his Tesla Model S ploughed at 74 miles per hour into the side of a lorry which had turned across his path. It was calculated that Brown had at least ten seconds to react, but neither he nor the Tesla's semi-autonomous "Autopilot" system made any attempt to brake to avoid the collision. It seems the system, which controlled speed, lane position and braking, failed to detect the white side of the truck's trailer against the background of sky. Brown had his hands on the steering wheel for a total of 25 seconds in a 37-minute trip, despite six audible warnings from the car that he had spent too long with his hands off the wheel.

The US National Transportation Safety Board concluded that "operational" limitations in the Autopilot system played a major role in the crash. Whilst Brown was blamed for not paying attention and for being excessively reliant on the Autopilot system's capabilities, Tesla were criticised for designing a system that was too easy to misuse. Autopilot didn't do enough to ensure a driver was paying adequate attention; it allowed a driver to avoid steering or looking at the road ahead for lengthy periods of time at high speeds and on roads other than the type for which it was designed (highways and other limited-access roads). The system could not reliably detect cross-traffic like the truck in front of Brown.

Joshua Brown's crash illustrates a number of issues thrown up by current developments in automotive technology. The next couple of decades will be an exciting but very challenging time, not just for the automotive industry but for society in general, because the technological changes that are happening as we move towards "driverless" cars are likely to have enormous social ramifications. Imagine a world in which ill-health, disability and age are no barriers to mobility; robot vehicles transport goods and services from manufacturer to customer; and road-accident rates are a fraction of what they are at present, because their major cause (human error) has been eliminated. We seem to be heading towards a truly utopian world. However, as well as benefits, technological change usually brings problems which need to be addressed. This chapter will discuss some of the issues surrounding the development of driver-assistance systems and "driverless" vehicles.

THE MANY LEVELS OF "DRIVERLESS CARS"

Before we begin, we really need to be clear about what we are talking about, because the term *driverless cars* has been applied to a wide variety of systems, from cars with driver-assistance systems to fully self-driving vehicles. The Society of Automotive Engineers has devised a useful classification system (SAE J3016) with six levels.

Most existing cars are at levels 0 or 1; the driver does all or part of the driving. At level 0, the driver has full control. A level 1 vehicle has "driver-assistance"; most functions are controlled by the driver, but the car handles a specific function (either speed, braking or steering). Level 1 features are now appearing in mass-market cars. Adaptive cruise control maintains a constant target speed, differing from conventional cruise control in that it also adjusts the vehicle's speed, for example slowing in order to keep a safe distance from any vehicles ahead and then returning to the target speed once the way ahead is clear. Autonomous emergency braking systems warn the driver and then automatically apply the brakes to avoid a collision with any obstacles ahead. Automatic lane maintenance systems detect the lane markings and ensure that the vehicle remains between them.

Level 2 vehicles, with "partial driving automation", are now becoming available. Here, the car controls both speed and steering, but the driver does the rest of the driving and is supposed to supervise what the system is doing. Volvo, BMW and Mercedes all have systems available, though they are not as sophisticated as Tesla's Autopilot.

In levels 3 to 5, the car performs all of the driving. In level 3, "conditional driving automation", the car drives itself, but the driver is expected to be ready to take control if the system fails or cannot cope with the driving demands. Many manufacturers, including Volvo and Ford, have said they will skip level 3 altogether, because of the likelihood that drivers would become dangerously over-reliant on the system and cease to monitor it satisfactorily.

The term *driverless car* really refers only to vehicles at levels 4 and 5, where the driver is merely a passenger (or not in the vehicle at all). At these levels, the person in the vehicle is not expected to intervene if the system cannot cope; the vehicle should achieve a "minimal risk condition", such as slowly limping home or coming to a halt in a safe place. Level 4 is "high driving automation", and level 5 is "full driving automation". The main difference between these two levels is that the level 4 vehicle would be expected to operate within a specific environment (for example relying on adequate GPS coverage, clear lane markings, and so on), whereas the level 5 vehicle would be more versatile, able to drive wherever a vehicle might travel under the control of a human (across the Gobi Desert, for example).

Essentially, we have two qualitatively different sets of task demands here. Levels 1 to 3 free the driver from operating the controls of the car to varying extents, but the driver is required to monitor the situation, in theory being ready to step in if anything goes wrong. Levels 4 and 5 are quite different; the driver is merely a passenger in a robot taxi, and the only thing that is required of him or her is to have faith that the vehicle will be able to cope with whatever traffic situations it might encounter.

ISSUES WITH "SEMI-AUTONOMOUS" VEHICLES

Semi-autonomous vehicles like Brown's Tesla (levels 1 to 3) use "driver-assistance" systems to relieve the driver of most of the "operational"-level demands of driving. The driver has to pay little or no attention to accelerating, braking and steering. The assumption is that this will make driving easier, less mentally demanding and less fatiguing. Unfortunately, psychological research suggests that "driver-assistance" systems are likely to cause more problems than they solve.

For several decades, human factors experts, such as Neville Stanton and his group at the University of Southampton, have been highlighting the potential dangers posed by driver-assistance systems. They point out that semi-autonomous systems fundamentally change the nature of the driver's task, from active engagement in driving to passive monitoring of the vehicle's status. The designers of these systems expect that drivers will continually monitor the systems' performance, ready to resume control at a moment's notice if necessary. However, this is quite unrealistic. For one thing, the need for constant surveillance makes the automation largely pointless; if you still need your mind on the road in case something goes wrong, then why not drive anyway? The reality is that humans are pretty poor at vigilance tasks like this. They have a limited attention span (20 minutes or so, as opposed to the hours of supervision required for a typical journey), and they are easily distracted. Also, we have already seen how many drivers falsely believe they can avoid "wasting" the time spent in driving by trying to combine it with other tasks, such as using a mobile phone or texting (see Chapter 2). In semi-autonomous vehicles, many drivers will be sorely tempted by in-car distractions, such as phones, newspapers, DVD players and the like. If not distracted, they may be asleep. Even a conscientious driver is likely to lose Situation Awareness, both for what is happening outside the car and for the state of the vehicle's own systems.

The primary argument for introducing semi-autonomous systems is that they will lessen the processing demands on the driver. This in itself is arguable, since having to monitor the performance of the automated systems as well as monitoring the environment for hazards may actually *increase* the driver's workload. Research on information-processing has tended to focus on how performance is impaired by mental "overload", when processing demands exceed available mental resources. However mental underload may be just as undesirable. Malleable Attentional Resources Theory (MART) (Young and Stanton 2002) proposes that processing resources actually shrink in response to a lack of demand for them. In a semi-autonomous vehicle, the driver will be in a state of mental underload. In an emergency, the driver will be faced with a rapid increase in demand for processing resources – but will have even fewer resources available than a driver who is not being "assisted" by these systems.

MART is supported by a number of driving simulator experiments looking at what happens when an automated system fails unexpectedly, leaving the driver to retake control. As long as twenty years ago, Stanton and his colleagues showed that drivers might not cope effectively under these conditions. When an adaptive cruise control system failed to respond to a vehicle ahead by slowing down, a third of their participants were unable to avoid a collision.

Eriksson and Stanton (2017b) reviewed drivers' response times under various conditions. Level 0 drivers took 1 second to respond to sudden events in traffic. Drivers with adaptive cruise control and steering assistance took an extra 1.1 to 1.5 seconds to respond to a sudden automation failure. Drivers of highly automated vehicles (like Brown's Tesla) took 3 seconds or more to respond to a request by the car for them to resume manual control in an emergency. Peter Hancock, another expert in this field, summed up the situation pithily: "If you build systems where people are rarely required to respond, they will rarely respond when required".

Emergencies are not the only time when the driver would be expected to regain control of a highly automated car; at present, the systems are only supposed to be used under circumscribed conditions, such as motorways, so drivers should be regularly switching between assisted and unassisted driving. Using a Tesla on real roads, Eriksson, Banks and Stanton (2017) found that the mean takeover time was 3 seconds, but there was a long tail, with some drivers taking as long as 15 seconds.

Even if driver-assistance systems do their job well, there is the risk that they can divorce the driver from how the vehicle is performing, especially if the driver lacks knowledge about the performance limits of the system concerned. The psychological theory of "mental models" is relevant here (Stanton and Young, 2000). A mental model is the user's conception of how a system operates, based on knowledge, inferences and analogies with previous experiences. Difficulties arise when the user's mental model differs from that of the system's designer. To give you an example, I hired a car with a "handbrake" button on the dashboard. Every time I stopped, I pushed the button to apply the handbrake. I pushed the button again before moving off to release the handbrake – and stalled the car every time. Once I got home and read the handbook, I found out why the car was stalling. I had applied my "mental model" of handbrake operation, based on my past experiences of mechanical handbrakes – you apply it once stopped and release it to pull away. The designer's mental model was of a handbrake that you applied yourself (by pushing the button) but which automatically released itself when the car moved forwards. Every time I tried to move off, the car was helpfully releasing the handbrake and I was pushing the button to turn it back on again!

This was perplexing rather than dangerous, but serious problems could arise from inappropriate mental models of vehicle systems. Sometimes these can be "mode confusions", where the driver thinks the vehicle is in a different state from what it actually is. Many cars and motorcycles now have different selectable setups for suspension, braking and engine performance. Problems are likely to occur if a driver charges into a bend in the mistaken belief that the suspension is in firm "sports" mode, when it's actually in a more wallowy "touring" mode or if a motorcyclist accelerates hard on a wet road, forgetting that he or she is in full-power "sport" mode rather than detuned "rain" mode. The existence of different performance modes may make it difficult for the user to become fully familiar with the vehicle's characteristics in terms of handling and power delivery.

Designers need to ensure that drivers have an appropriate mental model of how their vehicle operates and how it will respond to their actions. Designers also need to consider how drivers are likely to try to apply their existing mental models to new technological innovations (as in the case of the handbrake example earlier). For almost a century, cars have shared a highly standardised control system. Vehicle controls are now becoming not only more complicated but more diverse between manufacturers. Up to now, vehicle control has been primarily to do with the skills of steering, acceleration and clutch control. An increasingly important component of driver education in the future will be to ensure drivers fully comprehend what "driver-assistance" systems can and cannot do.

This relates to the user's degree of trust in the systems. Excessive trust is obviously undesirable, leading to uncritical reliance on the technology, misuse and possibly accidents like Joshua Brown's. Excessive distrust means drivers won't use the system even when they could do so safely. The driver's degree of trust needs to be accurately calibrated to the system's objective level of reliability, as no system is foolproof. Trust is influenced not only by the system's reliability but also by factors such as the extent to which drivers think they are more competent than the system and their mental model of the system.

ISSUES WITH "DRIVERLESS" VEHICLES

Completely driverless vehicles (levels 4 and 5) raise different issues. A big difficulty is trying to overcome a lack of public confidence in the safety of driverless vehicles. In a recent Ipsos MORI poll, only 28% of respondents agreed with the statement "I think fully self-driving cars are what we should be working towards". Only 13% said they would always use an autonomous driving function if one were available.

This distrust seems to stem from fears about cybersecurity and hacking, together with an inflated idea of human driving abilities relative to a computer's. Recall from Chapter 3 that human assessment of risk is quite irrational and highly influenced by extraneous factors.

Something is more likely to be considered "risky" if it is unfamiliar and outside of the person's control. Driverless cars will, at least initially, meet both of these criteria. Although driverless cars are likely to be very safe, especially compared to the average human driver, any accidents involving them will be highly publicised. Accidents involving human drivers will remain so commonplace that they will seldom get any publicity. The "availability heuristic" will mean that the public will be much more aware of the risks of driverless cars than of human drivers. The lack of control over driverless vehicles will also exaggerate their apparent riskiness in the minds of the public. It is interesting that few people would baulk at travelling in a taxi, a vehicle over which they also have no control and which is likely to be operated by a driver who may have had little sleep and who is trying to use a mobile phone, radio and satnav while driving. Familiarity with taxis reduces their perceived riskiness.

Driverless cars also raise the issue of driver de-skilling: people might pass their driving test and then never actually drive a vehicle again for years. Will driving licences need to be renewed every few years, perhaps in conjunction with re-testing or even re-training?

There will inevitably be a transition period, during which conventional and driverless cars will have to coexist. It is notable that the very few accidents involving Google's driverless car seem to have occurred because human road-users expected the car to behave like another human. One of the supposed benefits of driverless vehicles is that vehicle-to-vehicle communication will enable them to drive closer together, thus maximising the use of road space and improving fuel economy by slipstreaming. However, in a simulator study, Gouy et al. (2014) found that "platooning" automated trucks on a motorway had a bad influence on drivers of adjacent vehicles, encouraging them to adopt excessively short headways from the vehicle ahead of them.

The technology to date has largely focused on vehicle control (keeping in lane and avoiding bumping into things). A great deal of progress has been made at this "operational" level of driving, but as we have seen in earlier chapters, human driving involves much more than this. Humans use strategies, heuristics and schemas in order to drive because they simply cannot process information fast enough to manage otherwise. By using our experiences to guide our actions, we can overcome the limitations of a nervous system that is limited to transmitting information at a mere 100 metres per second (very sluggish compared to the speed of electricity in a computer). The "tactical" and "strategic" levels of driving are going to be much harder to automate.

Having said this, it may be that vehicles do not need to drive like humans do. Driverless cars will be able to react faster than humans, and they will be actively sharing information with each other. Also whereas humans rely primarily on a highly selective visual system, current driverless systems integrate information from a wide variety of sensors: radar, lidar sensors (that work by bouncing pulses of light off the surroundings), ultrasonic sensors and GPS. In theory, at least, this "redundancy" should enable vehicles to navigate under conditions where humans cannot. At present, the reality is that heavy rain defeats lidar, radar and conventional cameras. At the 2018 Consumer Electronics Show in Las Vegas, torrential rain prompted several car manufacturers to abandon their demonstrations of semi-autonomous vehicles. In fairness to the autonomous vehicles, these conditions defeat human visual systems too – witness the motorway pile-ups that have occurred because of drivers speeding in fog or heavy rain.

CONCLUSION

By eliminating human error, the major cause of road accidents, automated vehicles have the potential to greatly improve road safety. However, unregulated and ill-considered introduction of technology into vehicles means that road safety is quite likely to get worse before it gets better.

As Donald Norman pointed out nearly 30 years ago, many of the psychological problems posed by vehicle automation have already been encountered in the aviation industry (Norman, 1990). Plane crashes have taught aircraft manufacturers valuable lessons about designing human-machine interfaces. It seems that the automotive industry is failing to learn from the aviation industry's experiences. Early aircraft autopilot systems were of the "strong but silent" type: they grappled with escalating difficulties produced by bad weather or equipment failures until they could no longer cope, at which point they relinquished control back to the aircrew. By this time, the situation was often so bad that the aircrew were unable to deal with it either. Modern systems are more "chatty", keeping the aircrew informed of the plane's status, so that the crew can hopefully become aware of emerging problems and intervene before the situation becomes critical.

We already have cars with cruise control, electronic stability programmes, traction control, anti-lock brakes and "intelligent" suspension. These systems are what Stanton has called "vehicle automation": they assist the driver, but the decision-making remains fully under the driver's control. The latest technologies, such as adaptive cruise control, collision-avoidance and autonomous emergency braking, are qualitatively different. Stanton refers to these as "driver automation" because they are taking over some of the decision-making. These systems are of the "strong but silent" type: the driver may remain unaware of just how much the automation is doing behind the scenes until it loses control, generally at a point way beyond the average driver's level of ability. Eriksson and Stanton (2017a) argue that vehicle automation systems should be designed to be more communicative with drivers, keeping them informed of their status: more of a chatty co-pilot than a silent autopilot. This would have the additional benefit of reducing underload, by keeping the driver more engaged with what the vehicle is doing.

Pilots have the advantage that they are usually flying at 35,000 feet, which buys them some time to get back "into the loop", reacquire Situation Awareness and hopefully perform corrective actions to solve a problem. Drivers do not have the luxury of time; by the time they have realised the vehicle's systems can no longer cope, it will almost certainly be too late to do anything about it, especially if averting disaster would require driving skills that have lapsed through disuse (or perhaps have never been acquired in the first place, if the driver has only ever driven high-tech cars).

In March 2017, Miltos Kyriakidis and eleven other human factors experts published their views on the challenges posed by autonomous vehicles. While acknowledging that autonomous vehicles have huge potential for increasing road safety, the experts were united in their concerns that automation was being introduced with apparently little regard for the human factors aspects. Drivers were being left "out of the loop" by the automation, but expected to intervene when the systems failed to cope. The article ends on what is almost a note of despair:

> It may be argued that our concerns and recommendations hardly differ from early HF [human factors] lessons learned from aviation and other automation domains . . . For example, an early report on HF for future air traffic control stated: "men, on the whole, are poor monitors. We suggest that great caution be exercised in assuming that men can successfully monitor complex automatic machines and 'take over' if the machine breaks down" (Fitts 1951) . . . Why HF researchers seem to convey the same message for decades is a question that deserves further consideration.
>
> (Kyriakidis et al. 2017, p. 15)

Peter Hancock makes a similar point: until truly driverless vehicles arrive, it's vital that designers of automated systems take into account the driver's psychology, rather than treating the human as a "subsystem of last resort" (Hancock, 2014). The driver is not a component of the system that can be marginalised until something goes wrong with the automation. If vehicle designers continue to ignore this fact, the car manufacturers' utopian vision of driving in the future is unlikely to materialise.

Throughout this book, I hope to have convinced you that psychological theory and research have something very useful to say about many aspects of driving. We may be moving into an era where humans are less involved in the physical actions of vehicle control, but until vehicles dispense with humans altogether, an understanding of the psychology of driving will be just as relevant to driver safety in the future as it is today.

FURTHER READING

USEFUL BOOKS

Banks, V.A. and Stanton, N.A. (2017). *Automobile automation: Distributed cognition on the road.* London: CRC Press.

Bédard, H. and Delashmit, G. (2011). *Accidents: causes, analysis and prevention.* New York: Nova.

Fisher, D.L., Caird, J., Horrey, W. and Trick, L. (eds.) (2016). *Handbook of teen and novice drivers: research, practice, policy and directions.* London: CRC Press.

Groeger, J. (2016). *Understanding driving: Applying cognitive psychology to a complex everyday task.* London: Routledge. (Actually the paperback version of a book published in 2000, so a little dated; but still worth reading).

Hennessy, D. (ed.) (2011). *Traffic psychology: An international perspective.* New York: Nova.

Hilbert, R.C. (ed.) (2011). *Distracted driving.* New York: Nova.

Jiménez, F. (ed.) (2018). *Intelligent vehicles, 1st edition: Enabling technologies and future developments.* Oxford: Butterworth-Heinemann.

Norman, D. (2013). *The design of everyday things: Revised and expanded edition.* New York: Basic Books. (Not specifically on driving, but it discusses the psychology of design and so covers issues that are highly relevant to driving).

Porter, B.E. (ed.) (2011). *Handbook of traffic psychology, 1st edition.* London: Academic Press. (Chapters on all aspects of transport psychology).

Shinar, D. (2017). *Traffic safety and human behavior* (2nd. edition.). Bingley: Emerald Publishing.

USEFUL WEB RESOURCES

IAM Roadsmart often commission research on various issues relating to the psychology of driving. have a look at their website: www.iamroadsmart.com/ and in particular their archive of well-conducted and very readable research reports, at www.iamroadsmart.com/media-and-policy/research-and-policy/archive

ROSPA (the Royal Society for the Prevention of Accidents) has some useful research-based information on its website: www.rospa.com/road-safety/advice/drivers/

REFERENCES

ACEM. (2009). *MAIDS: In-depth investigations of accidents involving powered two wheelers. Final report 2.0.* Retrieved 13/2/2018, from *www.maids-study.eu/pdf/MAIDS2.pdf*

Amado, S., Arikan, E., Kaca, G., Koyuncu, M. and Turkan, B.N. (2014). How accurately do drivers evaluate their own driving behavior? An on-road observational study. *Accident Analysis and Prevention, 63,* 65–73.

Arnett, J.J. (1996). Sensation seeking, aggressiveness and adolescent reckless behavior. *Personality and Individual Differences, 20*(6), 693–702.

Atchley, P., Tran, A.V. and Salehinejad, M.A. (2017). Constructing a publically available distracted driving database and research tool. *Accident Analysis and Prevention, 99,* 306–311.

Ball, K. and Owsley, C. (1992). The useful field of view test: A new technique for evaluating age-related declines in visual function. *Journal of the American Optometrist Association, 63,* 71–79.

Benfield, J.A., Szlemko, W.J. and Bell, P.A. (2007). Driver personality and anthropomorphic attributions of vehicle personality relate to reported aggressive driving tendencies. *Personality and Individual Differences, 42*(2), 247–258.

Briggs, G.F., Hole, G.J. and Land, M.F. (2016). Imagery-inducing distraction leads to cognitive tunnelling and deteriorated driving performance. *Transportation Research Part F, 38,* 106–117.

Brown, S.L. and Cotton, A. (2003). Risk-mitigating beliefs, risk estimates and self-reported speeding in a sample of Australian drivers. *Journal of Safety Research, 34,* 183–188.

Cavallo, V. and Pinto, M. (2012). Are car daytime running lights detrimental to motorcycle conspicuity? *Accident Analysis and Prevention*, 49, 78–85.

Chapman, P. and Underwood, G. (2000). Forgetting near-accidents: The role of severity, culpability and experience in the poor recall of dangerous driving situations. *Applied Cognitive Psychology*, 14, 31–44.

Clarke, S. and Robertson, I.T. (2005). A meta-analytic review of the big five personality factors and accident involvement in occupational and non-occupational settings. *Journal of Occupational and Organizational Psychology*, 78, 355–376.

Davison, P. and Irving, A. (1980). Survey of visual acuity of drivers, *TRRL Report* 945, Transport and Road Research Laboratory, Crowthorne, Berkshire.

Dahlen, E.R., Martin, R.C., Ragan, K. and Kuhlman, M. (2005). Driving anger, sensation seeking, impulsiveness and boredom proneness in the prediction of unsafe driving. *Accident Analysis and Prevention*, 37, 341–348.

Deffenbacher, J.L., Huff, M.E., Lynch, R.S., Oetting, E.R., and Salvatore, N.F. (2000). Characteristics and treatment of high-anger drivers. *Journal of Counselling Psychology*, 47(1), 5–17.

Department for Transport. (2017). *Reported road casualties in Great Britain: 2016 annual report.* Retrieved 13/2/2018 from *www.gov.uk/government/statistics/reported-road-casualties-great-britain-annual-report-2016*

De Winter, J.C.F. and Dodou, D. (2010). The driver behaviour questionnaire as a predictor of accidents: A meta-analysis. *Journal of Safety Research*, 41(6), 463–470.

Dobbs, A.R., Heller, R.B. and Schopflocher, D. (1998) A comparative approach to identify unsafe older drivers. *Accident Analysis and Prevention*, 30(3), 363–370.

Drummer, O.H., Gerostamoulos, J., Batziris, H., Chu, M., Caplehorn, J., Robertson, M.D. and Swann, P. (2004). The involvement of drugs in drivers of motor vehicles killed in Australian road traffic crashes. *Accident Analysis and Prevention*, 36(2), 239–248.

Dula, C.S. and Ballard, M.E. (2003). Development and evaluation of a measure of dangerous, aggressive, negative emotional and risky driving. *Journal of Applied Social Psychology*, 33(2), 263–282.

Duncan, J., Williams, P. and Brown, I. (1991). Components of driving skill: Experience does not mean expertise. *Ergonomics*, 34, 919–937.

Eriksson, A., Banks, V.A. and Stanton, N.A. (2017). Transition to manual: Comparing simulator with on-road control transitions. *Accident Analysis and Prevention*, 102, 227–234.

Eriksson, A. and Stanton, N.A. (2017a). The chatty co-driver: A linguistics approach applying lessons learnt from aviation incidents. *Safety Science*, 99, 94–101.

Eriksson, A. and Stanton, N.A. (2017b). Takeover time in highly automated vehicles: Noncritical transitions to and from manual control. *Human Factors*, 59(4), 689–705.

Fernandes, R., Job, R.F.S. and Hatfield, J. (2007). A challenge to the assumed generalizability of prediction and countermeasure for risky driving: Different factors predict different risky driving behaviors. *Journal of Safety Research*, 38, 59–70.

Fitts, P.M. (1951). *Human engineering for an effective air-navigation and traffic-control system.* Washington, DC: National Research Council.

Gouy, M., Wiedemann, K., Stevens, A., Brunett, G. and Reed, N. (2014). Driving next to automated vehicle platoons: How do short time headways influence non-platoon drivers' longitudinal control? *Transportation Research Part F*, 27, 264–273.

Greaves, S.P. and Ellison, A.B. (2011). Personality, risk aversion and speeding: An empirical investigation. *Accident Analysis and Prevention*, 43(5), 1828–1836.

Hancock, P.A. (2014). Automation: how much is too much? *Ergonomics*, 57(3), 449–454.

Hancock, P.A., Lesch, M. and Simmons, L. (2003). The distraction effects of phone use during a crucial driving maneuver. *Accident Analysis and Prevention*, 35, 501–514.

Holland, C., Geraghty, J. and Shah, K. (2010). Differential moderating effect of locus of control on effect of driving experience in young male and female drivers. *Personality and Individual Differences*, 48, 821–826.

Horne, J.A. and Reyner, L.A. (1996). Counteracting driver sleepiness: Effects of napping, caffeine and placebo. *Psychophysiology*, 33, 306–309.

Hyman, Jr, I.E., Boss, S.M., Wise, B.M., McKenzie, K.E. and Caggiano, J.M. (2010). Did you see the unicycling clown? Inattentional Blindness while walking and talking on a cell phone. *Applied Cognitive Psychology*, 24, 597–607.

Johnson, C.A. and Keltner, J.L. (1983). Incidence of visual field loss in 20,000 eyes and its relationship to driving performance. *Archives of Ophthalmology*, 101, 371–375.

Jonah, B. (1997). Sensation seeking and risky driving: A review and synthesis of the literature. *Accident Analysis and Prevention*, 29(5), 651–665.

Kay, G.G. and Logan, B.K. (2011). *Drugged driving expert panel report: a consensus protocol for assessing the potential of drugs to impair driving.* (DOT HS 811 438). Washington, DC: National Highway Traffic Safety Administration.

Killoran, A., Cunning, U., Doyle, N. and Sheppard, L. (2010). *Review of effectiveness of laws limiting blood alcohol concentration levels to reduce alcohol-related road injuries and deaths.* Final Report March 2010. Centre for Public Health Excellence NICE.

Kyriakidis, M., de Winter, J.C.F., Stanton, N., Bellet, T., van Arem, B., Brookhuis, K., Martens, M.H., Bengler, K. Andersson, J., Merat, N., Reed, N., Flament, M., Hagenzieker, M. and Happee, R. (2017). A human factors perspective on automated driving, *Theoretical Issues in Ergonomics Science*, 1–27. Published online 8th March 2017.

Lajunen, T. (2001). Personality and accident liability: Are extraversion, neuroticism and psychoticism related to traffic and occupational fatalities? *Personality and Individual Differences*, 31, 1365–1373.

Lajunen, T. and Parker, D. (2001). Are aggressive people aggressive drivers? A study of the relationship between self-reported general aggressiveness, driver anger and aggressive driving. *Accident Analysis and Prevention*, 33, 243–255.

Langham, M., Hole, G., Edwards, J. and O'Neill, C. (2002). An analysis of "looked but failed to see" accidents involving parked police cars. *Ergonomics*, 45, 167–185.

Lesch, M.F. and Hancock, P.A. (2004). Driving performance during concurrent cell-phone use: Are drivers aware of their performance decrements? *Accident Analysis and Prevention*, 36(3), 471–480.

Lombardi, D., Horrey, W.J. and Courtney, T.K. (2017). Age-related differences in fatal intersection crashes in the United States. *Accident Analysis and Prevention*, 99, 20–29.

Magazzù, D., Comelli, M. and Marinoni, A. (2006). Are car drivers holding a motorcycle licence less responsible for motorcycle – car crash occurrence? A non-parametric approach. *Accident Analysis and Prevention*, 38, 365–370.

Marottoli, R.A. and Richardson, E.D. (1998). Confidence in and self-rating of, driving ability among older drivers. *Accident Analysis and Prevention*, 30(3), 331–336.

Maycock, G. (1997). Sleepiness and driving: The experience of U.K. car drivers. *Accident Analysis and Prevention*, 29(4), 453–462.

Moskowitz, H. and Fiorentino, D. (2000). *A review of the literature on the effects of low doses of alcohol on driving-related skills*. (DOT HS 809 028). Washington, DC: National Highway Traffic Safety Administration.

Musselwhite, C. (2006). Attitudes towards vehicle driving behaviour: Categorising and contextualising risk. *Accident Analysis and Prevention*, 38, 324–334.

Norman, D.A. (1990). The "problem" with automation: inappropriate feedback and interaction, not "over-automation". *Philosophical Transactions of the Royal Society of London, B: Bioogical Sciences*, 327(1241), 585–593.

Norman, D.A. and Shallice, T. (1986). Attention to action: Willed and automatic control of behavior. Pages 1–18 in Davidson, R., Schwartz, G. and Shapiro, D. (eds.), *Consciousness and self regulation: Advances in research and theory, Volume 4*. New York: Plenum.

Ramaekers, J.G., Berghaus, G., van Laar, M. and Drummer, O.H. (2004). Dose related risk of motor vehicle crashes after cannabis use. *Drug and Alcohol Dependence*, 73(2), 109–119.

Read, N., Kinnear, N. and Weaver, L. (2012). *Why do older drivers have more 'failed to look' crashes? A simulator based study*. Project Report PPR635. Berkshire: TRL.

Redelmeier, D.A. and Tibshirani, R.J. (1997). Association between cellular telephone calls and motor-vehicle collisions. *The New England Journal of Medicine*, 336, 453–458.

Road Safety Foundation. (n.d.). *Supporting safe driving into old age: A national older driver strategy*. Older Drivers Task Force. Retrieved 13/2/2018 from https://s3-eu-west-1.amazonaws.com/roadsafetyfoundation.org/2016-07-04_Older_drivers/2016-07-04_Older_drivers_02_report.pdf

Sagberg, F., Jackson, P., Krüger, H.P., Muzet, A. and Williams, A. (2004). *Fatigue, sleepiness and reduced alertness as risk factors in driving*. TOI report 739/2004. Oslo: Institute of Transport Economics.

Senaratna, C.V., Perret, J.L., Lodge, C.J., Lowe, A.J., Campbell, B.E., Matheson, M.C., Hamilton, G.S. and Dharmage, S.C. (2017). Prevalence of obstructive sleep apnea in the general population: a systematic review. *Sleep Medicine Reviews*, 34, 70–81.

Shinoda, H., Hayhoe, M.M. and Shrivastava, A. (2001). What controls attention in natural environments? *Vision Research*, 41, 3535–3545.

Simons, D.J. and Chabris, C.F. (1999). Gorillas in our midst: Sustained inattentional Blindness for dynamic events. *Perception*, 28, 1059–1074.

Stanton, N.A. and Young, M.S. (2000). A proposed psychological model of driving automation. *Theoretical Issues in Ergonomics Science*, 1, 315–331.

Stanton, N.A., Stewart, R., Harris, D., Houghton, R.J., Baber, C., McMaster, R., Salmon, P., et al. (2006). Distributed Situation Awareness in dynamic systems: theoretical development and application of an ergonomics methodology. *Ergonomics*, 49, 1288–1311.

Strayer, D. L., Watson, J. M. and Drews, F. A. (2011). Cognitive distraction while multitasking in the automobile. Pages 29–58, in Ross, B. (ed.), *The Psychology of Learning and Motivation, Volume* 54. Burlington: Academic Press.

Thiffault, P. and Bergeron, J. (2003). Monotony of road environment and driver fatigue: A simulator study. *Accident Analysis and Prevention*, 35, 381–391.

Tversky, A. and Kahneman, D. (1973). Availability: A heuristic for judging frequency and probability. *Cognitive Psychology*, 5, 207–232.

Ulleberg, P. (2002). Personality subtypes of young drivers. Relationship to risk-taking preferences, accident involvement, and response to a traffic safety campaign. *Transportation Research Part F*, 4, 279-297.

Vingilis, E. and Macdonald, S. (2002). Review: Drugs and traffic collisions. *Traffic Injury Prevention*, 3, 1–11.

World Health Organization. (2015). *Global status report on road safety 2015*. Geneva: WHO Press.

Young, M.S. and Stanton, N.A. (2002). Malleable Attentional Resources Theory: A new explanation for the effects of mental underload on performance. *Human Factors*, 44(3), 365–375.

Zhou, R., Yu, M. and Wang, X. (2016). Why do drivers use mobile phones while driving? The contribution of compensatory beliefs. *PLOS One*, 11(8), 1–18.

Zuckerman, M. (1994). *Behavioural expressions and biological bases of sensation seeking*. Cambridge: Cambridge University Press.